The Tarim Network recognises the ongoing struggles of yerlik (native) peoples globally, including those who are nationless and those still living on unceded land. We stand in solidarity with yerlik communities in their efforts to assert sovereignty, protect their culture and traditions, and secure their rights to land and self-determination. We acknowledge the unique and enduring relationship yerlik peoples have with their lands and waters, and the immense richness and diversity of yerlik cultures, knowledge and histories. We acknowledge the pain and trauma inflicted by colonisation and ongoing acts of violence, and recognise the need for continuous efforts towards reconciliation.

Under the Mulberry Tree:
A Contemporary Uyghur Anthology
(Revised Edition)

Published by The Tarim Network

Edited by Munawwar Abdulla, Sonya Imin,
Maidina Kadeer and Emily Zinkin.

Cover photograph by Camilla Dilshat.

Layout and design by Jodie Manning,
Shiffa Samad, and Eleanor Wilson.

ISBN: 979-8-218-15690-9

Printed and bound by Ingram Sparks.
While every effort has been made to ensure
consistency in printing and binding, there may
be slight variations in the final product due to
differences in printing methods and materials.

Correspondence should be addressed to:
Email: info@thetarimnetwork.com

Under the Mulberry Tree

A Contemporary Uyghur Anthology

Volume I

Introduction

Munawwar Abdulla
Sonya Imin
Maidina Kadeer

We began working on *Under the Mulberry Tree: A Contemporary Uyghur Anthology* in 2021 to respond to the ongoing oppression and genocide of the Uyghur people. It is now a creative collaboration by members of the diasporic Uyghur community to insert, highlight, and amplify our own stories. We began by hosting a series of writing, editing, and creative workshops to support contributors in developing their work. After going through submissions, by early 2022 we launched an online-only edition of this volume with successful in-person and online launch events. Shortly after we decided to create an extended edition for a physical book, responding to strong interest from both individuals and institutions. This revised edition offers additional translations, remarks from the contributors, and notes from our editorial team to provide added educational context. Now, after over two years of work, we are proud to share this new and improved volume with our readers.

The heart of this volume lies in the stories and memories of our contributors. Their experiences span across time and space, including both first and second-generation perspectives, making this anthology a unique cross section across a broad breadth of Uyghur life. Some are established poets, artists, and writers, while many others have never been published. While we did not ask for a central theme, it was clear as we organised submissions that memory appeared as a common thread in people's work. For Uyghurs in the diaspora, memory often manifests as a collective yearning for a home to which we no longer have access. In this volume, these experiences of memory are explored through engaging with Uyghur language and literature, re-imagining Uyghur visual culture, and reflecting on one's life through personal essays and photography. The memories elicited by these works are more than mere re-tellings of an event. Instead, they serve as a living testimony ready to be witnessed.

The written and visual testimony in this anthology is a snapshot of the present moment of the Uyghur experience. The sharing of memory is an act of testimony towards a specific lived reality, which for Uyghurs is currently under threat. French philosopher Gabriel Marcel defines testimony as bearing witness to suffering. Sharing one's testimony requires the acceptance of personal truth through an act of "self-gifting", which for us has materialised in this anthology. Testimony also connects us to authentic meaning and personal liberty by expressing deeper experiences of identity and being, or what Marcel refers to as the "I". Our anthology is a space where this "I" is recorded, testified, and witnessed. It is an exploration of spaces, places, and faces that continue to live with and through the memories of every one of our contributors. Between these pages, our contributors have explored the memories of their personal and collective experiences, creating a space where Uyghur voices and interests could be harboured and put at the forefront of our discourse. In this way, we are testifying before our community and the world, exploring the complexity of what it means to be Uyghur in contemporary society. Subsequently, as China continues its denial of the ongoing genocide against the Uyghur and Turkic communities, forms of testimonial memory serve as an active re-structuring of what is perceived to be truth in history.

As an editorial team of young Uyghur women, we are pleased to present our first volume as a starting introduction to Uyghur life, culture, and experience beyond the colonial gaze. For a larger part of Uyghur history, attention to our lives and story only appears when violence and unrest erupt under imperial and colonial conquest. In the process of reflecting on our own lived realities, and the realities shared in this anthology, we recognise the vulnerability which comes from sharing and identifying the burdens that we often carry. Many in the diaspora have lost access to our homes and loved ones, and we continue to struggle in finding ways to channel that grief. Yet, this vulnerability of sharing our collective experiences, with both the hopes and the sorrows, has been able to paint an intimate reflection of Uyghur life. As much as this volume testifies to our struggles, it also gestures towards a resilience that we have continued to carry. The expansive power embedded in the encounters of art and literature allows Uyghur experiences, and the being of our "I", to be witnessed by our readers. "Under the Mulberry Tree" is thus the meeting place where we share our stories with one another, seeing and witnessing these creative manifestations of our memories.

The editorial team deeply thanks each of our contributors for trusting us with their work, as well as the Rene Cassin Institute and Moishe House who have continued to offer vital support throughout the development and publication processes.

The transliteration of Uyghur words in this anthology have not been italicised. By presenting Uyghur words without emphasis, the anthology attempts to reflect the natural linguistic blend that occurs in diaspora communities and make the content more relatable to readers who are familiar with this phenomenon.

Foreword

Emily Zinkin

This anthology is intended to lift up the stories and voices of the Uyghur people in celebration of their rich and diverse culture and individuality. Whilst it was created with the hope of raising awareness of the current genocide and as a call to action, it is also a celebration of the unique and varied identities, views and thoughts of the Uyghur diaspora, as a people who deserve to be heard and recognised for themselves.

Working with Sonya, Munawwar and Maidina, as well as all of our facilitators, has been an absolute pleasure, and it has been such a joy to programme and facilitate inter-faith creative workshops with them and the Moishe House Clapham community. It felt important to creatively connect a diasporic community known predominantly for being victims of a genocide with another who have experienced and survived their own, the Jewish community I'm part of. We spoke at length about the importance of the experience being shared, but also of it not being the only facet of our identity we are known for.

I began this project as a René Cassin Human Rights Ambassador wondering what I could do to help in some small way, and was excited when Mia Hassenson, the Director, suggested I used my skills as a writer and editor, but knew I needed to find a way to make Uyghur voices heard rather than speaking for them. When I was put in touch with the Tarim Network and we discussed the idea of an anthology I immediately felt excited about what we could achieve together, and that excitement hasn't dwindled in the many months we have worked on this project.

Every piece of work shared with us, via submissions, social media and in workshops has been a pleasure to experience. Thank you to everyone who participated, and I'm so excited this anthology exists to celebrate our contributors. May the future bring an end to the genocide, and may many more Uyghur creatives be published and celebrated.

A year on, and I am thrilled this project continues to move forward. I remember sending the front cover design to my fellow editors when we were finalising the original version of this anthology and being asked to add "Volume 1" to it, and here we are approaching a new version of the first volume and a second one! I couldn't have imagined it when I tentatively approached the Tarim Network with the idea and it has grown beyond what I could have dreamt of, with a widening community within an already international diaspora. We will continue our aim to uplift Uyghur voices and art, and I have no doubt this project will continue on to bigger and better things.

The geographic location of East Turkistan makes it an ideal climate for fruit farming. The southern region is most known for its grapes, notably the seedless white manaizi. Central and northern regions produce apples, pomegranates (anar), mulberries, and apricots, amongst other fruits. Traditional Uyghur homes often have large courtyards with trees that produce fruit, nuts, and flowers.

Untitled

Maidina Kadeer

If I lived in a country that recognised and respected me, I'd be in my
ay-mummam's garden, her head resting on my lap and the mountain
air caressing our skin in sweet tenderness. I'd see the roses bloom in
tones of red and purple, I'd serve Anars that poured like jewels we
no longer hid and the downward streams of its juices on our palms
would wash us away from yesterday. And when it rains it would pour
and my grandma would say a wolf was born, the thunder it's doula
and the earth it's mother.

*Ay-mummam translates to "my moon grandmother". Ay is the
Uyghur word for moon, and is often used in Uyghur women's
names. Gül, or flower, is another common word added to the
end of a name, often as a sign of endearment. These are just
two examples of naturalistic elements used in Uyghur names.*

Köyümchan

Aykezar Adil

Ésingizdimu momingizning öyining hidi?
Hem bowingizning shiwirlap qilghan du'aliri?
Ésingizdimu rohingizgha keshtilen'gen muhebbet?
Hem dunyagha bériwatqan méhringizning asasi?
Emesmusiz özingiz del shu momingizning öyi?

Do you remember the smell of your grandmother's home,
and the gentle whispers of your grandfather's prayers?
Do you remember the love that rooted itself in you, there?
Do you remember the reason you pour kindness into the world?
Do you remember that you are your grandmother's home?

ئېسىڭىزدىمۇ، مومىڭىزنىڭ ئۆيىنىڭ ھىدى؟

ھەم بوۋىڭىزنىڭ شىۋىرلاپ قىلغان دۇئالىرى؟

ئېسىڭىزدىمۇ، روھىڭىزغا كەشتىلەنگەن مۇھەببەت؟

ھەم دۇنياغا بېرىۋاتقان مېھرىڭىزنىڭ سەۋەبى ؟

ئەمەسمۇ، سىز دەل شۇ مومىڭىزنىڭ ئۆيى؟

Conversation with Contributor

AA *This poem was originally written in English with the intention of capturing the universal experience of grandmotherly love for readers. For Uyghur readers, the poem aims to remind them of the caring and loving roots from which they come. The text has been translated into both Uyghur Perso-Arabic and modern Latin scripts.*

The inclusion of two scripts serves to ensure that the poem can be read by most Uyghur readers. As a global population, many Uyghurs around the world use the Latin script, but there are ongoing efforts to teach and maintain the Perso-Arabic (UEY) script. A modified Latin script was initially adopted in 1959 (UYY) and standardised in the 2000s (ULY). However, the Perso-Arabic script remains the primary form of literary communication in East Turkistan, and most important religious, cultural, and historical Uyghur texts are written in this script. In recent years, scholars have worked tirelessly to translate these texts for the purpose of inclusion and cultivation among the global Uyghur community.

In addition to the Uyghur Perso-Arabic and modern Latin scripts, the Uyghur Cyrillic alphabet (USY) is also used by Uyghur populations in Kazakhstan and other Central Asian countries. Historically, the multitude of scripts has been a major hurdle for communication between different Uyghur and Turkic populations.

Bread, Tonur and Uyghur

*Muyesser Abdul'ehed
(Hendan)*

Uyghur bakes bread in Istanbul,
the dough of that bread kisses the tonur it touches.
A thoroughly cooked bread bakes Uyghur
the dough of that Uyghur is far, so far
burning in the heat of abandonment.

A tonur bakes bread in Istanbul,
it knows how to bake like my mother's tonur.
A bread bakes a tonur,
A bread knows how to find bread,
it asks to live, it has no stomach.

I am a piece of bread
that knows how to be baked.
I am a tonur
that knows how to bake.
I am an Uyghur
cutting my lips on bread,
baking in a tonur-like world,
in whose heart bread enters and falls.

I have entered the tonur,
I am done, the world can devour me,
they've chewed and spit me out, okay, that's fine.
Eh, I am bread,
Just Uyghur's bread
liked only by Uyghurs,
bled only by Uyghurs.

Bread like the sun, like the full moon,
left in a tonur in the Teklimakan,
rising each dawn and each dusk...

19 December 2017

Bread in Uyghur is called naan, tonur naan, or toqatch, and also has a variety of names for more specific types of bread. In the diaspora, Uyghur bakers (naway) in Türkiye continue the tradition of making bread the traditional way in a tonur. In the 1940s, East Turkistan faced the highest levels of impoverishment compared to inner China. During this time, naan was considered a poor man's food. The Uyghur phrase "nan bilen issiq chay" (naan and hot tea) refers to the significance of naan as a primary

نان، تونۇر ۋە
ئۇيغۇر

سۇيەسسەر ئابدۇللەھەد
(خەندر(ن))

نان ياقىدۇ ئىستانبۇلدا بىر ئۇيغۇر،
ناننىڭ خېمىرى يېنىدىكى تونۇرنى سۆيەر.
ئۇيغۇرنى ياقىدۇ سىڭىپ پىشقان نان،
ئۇيغۇرنىڭ خېمىرى يىراق بەك يىراق
تەرىك يېتىملىكنىڭ تەپتىدە كۆيەر.

نان ياقىدۇ ئىستانبۇلدا بىر تونۇر،
ئاپامنىڭ تونۇرىدەك نان يېقىشنى بىلەر.
تونۇرنى ياقىدۇ بىر نان،
نان تۆرۈپ نان تېپىشنى بىلەر،
قورسىقى يوق، جان بېقىشنى تىلەر.

مەن– بىر نان
يېقىلىشنى بىلمەيدىغان.
مەن– بىر تونۇر
يېقىشنى بىلمەيدىغان.
مەن– بىر ئۇيغۇر
نان لەۋلەرىنى تىلمەيدىغان،
تونۇردەك بىر دۇنيادا يېقىلمايدىغان،
نان كۆرۈپ يۈرىكىدە يېقىلمايدىغان...

مەن تونۇرغا كۆرۈپ كەتتىم،
پىشىپ چىقتىم، يېپىسۇن دۇنيا،
چىشلەپ تاشلىدى، مەيلى، بوپتۇلا.
ئىھ، نانمەن،
ئۇيغۇرنىڭ نېنىممەن پەقەت
دۇنيادا ئۇيغۇرغىلا ياقىدىغان،
ئۇيغۇرنىڭ قېنىدىلا ئاقىدىغان...

قۇياشتەك نانمەن، تولۇن ئايدەك نانمەن،
تەكلىماكاندا قالغان تونۇردا
ھەر سەھەر، ھەر ئاخشام ئاتىدىغان...

2017-يىلى 19-دېكابىر

source of nutrition for many impoverished Uyghurs. For Uyghurs, naan is
not only a core of Uyghur cuisine, but also symbolises a history of class
struggle. Naan continues to play a central role in guest culture in our
communities.

Stanley Toops "The Population Landscape of Xinjiang/East Turkistan"
(Inner Asia, 2000).

Toqatch

Ayesha Erkin

Toqatch is an Uyghur and Uzbek flatbread. It's a very common market bread in Turkic countries with vendors selling it fresh from the tandoor. It's a yeast-free bread, with little moisture so it stays fresh for a good while. The edges are thick, a little hard and brushed with oil, and sprinkled with white and black sesame seeds before baking.

The middle is softer and flatter, stamped with a circular pattern from a chekküch (or tamgha or tükche) which is a wooden and metal bread stamp. Stamping it keeps the dough from rising while cooking, but sometimes, certain patterns can be used to differentiate bakers in a market.

Hiraeth

Manzire

"Weten" means "homeland" and is often used to refer to home without invoking a political stance.

I don't dream about my family or weten that much, but I used to keep note whenever they appeared in my dreams in case I forgot the scene of being with my family.

There is the same fear of being taken away, being seen, being heard by the police in every single dream. And there is the same dilemma: my conscious voice is telling me, "It's okay, this is just a dream, just wake up and it will be over," while my subconscious is saying, "It's okay, it's just a dream, you won't be taken away, please don't wake up, just be with your family for one more minute."

‹ Notes　　　

20201111
梦到爸妈弟弟爷爷出国 在根特
我和他们在 Friday market 买鱼，爷爷坐在
轮椅上 我很伤心他们之前没告诉我这件事
但很开心我们在一个我可以保护他们的地
方 我带他们逛了根特 怎么会这么幸福？？
is this real?

20201111
Dreamed father, mother, my younger brother, and grandfather were abroad in Ghent. I was buying fish with them at the Friday Market. Grandfather was in a wheelchair. I was very sad they never told me about this before, but I was happy that we were somewhere where I could protect them. I showed them around Ghent. How come there is so much happiness?? Is this real?

Translation | Tumaris Yalqun

20210524
梦到在家 午休我爸给我补鞋子 好像还
送我 上学

20210707
梦到回家 我和爸妈弟弟逛超市 好高级
的超 市哦 进门处就有水果

The "pinyin" style of spelling in the original notes have been kept as is.

20210909
梦到我妈（好像）大家都在焉耆 qong oy
我 问我妈要湿巾 要补救一下我的我眼妆
我妈 看了看我的眼影 然后翻了翻包 说
没有了只 剩下擦过手的你用吗

20210524

Dreamed I was home. My father was fixing my shoes during lunch break. It seems like he also brought me to school.

20210707

Dreamed I was home. My parents, my younger brother, and I were at a supermarket. What a fancy supermarket this is. There are fruits at the entrance.

20210909

Dreamed of my mother. (Seemingly) everyone was at my grandparents' in Qarasheher. I asked for wet wipes from my mother. I wanted to refresh my eye makeup. My mum looked at my eye shadow. She searched for her purse. Told me she doesn't have any but there is one left from when she wiped her hands. She asked me if I still wanted to use it.

Translation | Mirshad Ghalip

20220210/4:14am

梦到我爸 qarsha chong oy 我在 ixkak oy 窗户前面蹲着马步看电脑刷微 博看到了杨紫的热搜：杨紫失忆。 我爸在外面启动车子是小时候的 qar santana 天气很好 有太阳 是焉耆的经典天 气 土里土气的 gherip 阳光普照，我爸要走 了大家都在外面送他 我没出去 大家开始 喊我名字让我出来跟我爸说再见 我不想出 来 没出来 我心里想我不想说再见我不要告 别我不要出去跟我爸告别 大家叫的越来越 大声 声音越大越可怕 很压迫感 我慌的开始 大哭 哭到被自己的哭声吵醒 稍微清醒起来发现没见着我爸 就哭的更厉 害了 怎么这么草率就醒了呀傲娇 likqip 我 爸没见到还给自己吵醒了 早知道就出去送 送他了 那还可以见他一面 说不定他只是去 lishxo 抓个鱼就回来了 并不是多久的分离

20220210/4:14am

Dreamed my father was at grandparents' place in Qarasheher. I was squatting by the window of another room, scrolling Weibo while watching TV. I saw YangZi trending on hot search: YangZi lost her memory. My father was starting a car outside, it was the black Santana from my childhood. The weather was great, sun was out. It was the typical weather of Qarasheher. The nostalgic lonely sun was covering everywhere. My dad was leaving, everyone was seeing him out. I didn't go outside, they started to call my name telling me to come out and say goodbye to my father. I didn't want to go outside. I didn't go. In my heart, I was thinking I don't want to say goodbye, I don't want to go out to say goodbye to my father. They started to call my name louder and louder. The louder the noise, the scarier it got. I felt pressured, I panicked and started crying until I woke myself up with loud cries. When my head grew clearer, I realised my father was not here with me and cried even more. How did I just wake up so sloppily, I shouldn't have acted so delicate. I didn't get to see my father and on top of that I woke myself up crying. If I knew, I would have gone out to say goodbye. Maybe he was only going to Lishiho to quickly catch some fish and come back. It wouldn't have been a long separation.

Translation | Tumaris Yalqun

Conversation with Contributor

M   *This is a dream diary. They say in the blink of an eye, your dream is gone. So I take note. It's the stupidest and most helpless thing; to forget the time with your family over a blink.*

I don't dream about my family or weten a lot, generally 3-4 times a year. It's the only few minutes I can feel that I'm actually around them. I wish I could take photos of my dreams and print them out.

So I guess that's the inspiration — since technology does not allow me to take photos yet, I go old-school, I write it down.

At first, it was just for the sake of my memory. After two years it gained more meaning. Now the notes empower and inspire me somehow.

It reminds me that I have a family who I love, who I cannot let down. I think sometimes I forget to think about their love and how much their happiness means to me, because their actual presence/existence in my life is just too little. So when I read the notes (especially when I'm down) I'm like — god, I love them so much that I will work my ass off to protect them and their modest life, to make them feel happy and proud.

We have too many sad stories. I think my message would be to try not to get too sad because of its useless void, don't let its power crush you and pummel you.

[continued] I can't really translate this with good words: 动荡的时代里更需要耐力与想象力　沮丧之外还有一些可能. *[tr: Turbulent times require more patience and imagination. Besides distress, there are also possibilities].*

I wanna repeat this again, every time, no matter what the dream is about, there is the same horror and the fight between my conscious and subconscious voice that drives me crazy. So I always wake up so tired and angry.

And the tejirbe [tr: experience, lesson] is that, try to really wake up and get out of your bed once your head is clearer. If you fall asleep at this point you will never remember the dream again — blink theory.

Language education policy has increasingly been used as a tool for assimilating and marginalising Uyghur culture since the Chinese Communist Party took over in 1949. Despite decades of an official "bilingual" policy, Uyghur schools have been sidelined in favour of Mandarin language education. As a result, Chinese educated Uyghurs, or "minkaohan", may find it easier to write or express themselves in Chinese. Another manifestation of the policy is reflected in this piece, where the author uses Chinese pinyin to spell Uyghur words instead of ULY. Many Uyghurs in the diaspora are only now learning ULY spelling.

Since 2017, the CCP has banned Uyghur language instruction and closed Uyghur schools in violation of Chinese law and basic human rights provisions. Additionally, Uyghur-language books and media have been prohibited, and individuals caught promoting the Uyghur language can face punishment, including imprisonment.

Trees from Home

Elminur Mahpirof

My favourite trees are located in weten, in Ghulja. They lead to my grandfather's farm. I grew up visiting that place from since I can remember. Whenever I feel homesick, I look at this picture and think of this place, and I can hear the sounds of the birds and the towns people walking by, waiting to be close enough to say, "Salam."

What you can't see is the two rivers behind those trees. I was always too scared to swim in them as a child, but when I visited weten in 2016, I saw how small those rivers are, and couldn't fathom what I had been so scared of.

Eid Morning in Teklimakan

Ali Sibir

"Come on! Get up! We better set off soon. And you're not allowed to leave this house without having your morning tea. Got it?"

He nodded without opening his eyes. He's not a morning person, he's never been one. But it felt extra hard that day to rise before the sun. That's what they all did every bayram: wake up before the sun, before the rooster crows. His father would go pray at the mosque before they all set off to cross the desert to reach the Imam Asim shrine. It might sound like a harsh trip, but no, getting out of bed was the real challenge to him. What if he overslept? Would the rest of them leave him behind and go? That would never happen. "Mum would yank me out of bed and drag me across the desert!" he chuckled to himself.

"You awake yet? Come on!"

His mum was standing next to his bed. He could smell the samsa baking in the oven. He rolled out sluggishly.

"I washed your green shirt, it's in the bathroom, put that on. Here, this doppa will look good with your green shirt. You better be quick, come on!"

The early morning tea and samsa... How delicious! The other day, the women in his neighbourhood had all gathered at their place to make sangza. Sangza is sold at the market, bazaar, even on Taobao these days. But his mother would never let them buy it. That was fine. His mother's sangza was the most delicious anyway.

Bayram refers to festivities, and is a word commonly used in many Muslim communities. In Uyghurche it refers to both Islamic and non-Islamic holidays, from Eid to Nowruz. Bayram celebrations hold memories for Uyghurs within weten and in the diasporic community as an event of community bonding and intergenerational exchange. In recent years, many Islamic bayrams have been prohibited or only allowed with strict restrictions and state oversight.

"Dad's back! Let's go!!"

His little brother was clapping his hands, jumping up and down. His excitement about this trip was annoying. Well, cute and annoying at the same time. His mum handed him two plastic bags full of what felt like rocks.

"Ohh, what have you filled these with!?"

"Nothing much! Some mutton, samsa, göshnan, grapes, almonds, and a watermelon and…"

He'd already clomped out of the house. The list wasn't likely to end anytime soon. His mother always took pride in feeding other people at the shrine. She would see it as a form of praying, too. "I feed them, and Allah feeds us." She wasn't the most religious Muslim on earth, that's for sure. But she would never miss the shrine visit. "It's not easy for us to go on a pilgrimage to the house of Allah in Mecca. But some of our ancestors were the most beloved believers of Allah, so we go and pay homage to their houses, their shrines, and we hope our visit would be considered somewhat equal to Hajj." That's what his mother and all those women in the village believed.

Their house wasn't far from the desert, so they took two of their horses to load the bags on their backs. Of course, they would cross the desert on foot. That was the tradition. But it was fine. His father would tell stories about Imam Asim, his mother would hand out food and water as needed, and before they knew it, they would see the flags waving from atop the shrine. They weren't alone on this trip. He could see familiar faces near and far. Some were reciting prayers; some were walking in silence. Weird, this time he could hear some footfalls. The soft, crumbling sand of the desert should have absorbed the footfalls of both the people and the animals. He looked around to see if anyone else recognised the sound. No…

The Imam Asim shrine was a site dedicated to a Muslim man who is thought to have helped defeat the Buddhist kingdom that had ruled there over a thousand years ago. Devotees often prayed there during holidays for abundant harvests, good health, and so on. This would include tying strips of cloths carrying prayer messages on wooden posts, after which they would enjoy fairground amusements, food, and games around the site's edge. This site has now been demolished by the CCP along with many other mosques and holy sites.

It must have been an hour or so since they had left the house. "Halfway there!" yelled his father, whose hazel eyes were sparkling. His father had had a tough life. Upon losing his parents as a teenager, he'd had to drop out of school to start working at the blacksmith's in their village. To him, his father was an artist. He would hide in a corner in the tiny blacksmith shop and watch him work with metal for hours. His father wouldn't let him in the shop, fearing that he would fall behind on schoolwork. He wished he could have spent more time with his father — you know, some "man time" as father and son. His father had to work hard for long hours in the shop and would come home dead tired and head straight to bed. This trip to the shrine was the longest time he spent with his father every year.

He would be taking the gaokao, the college entrance exam, next year. All he wanted was to be placed in a good school. Maybe he would go to Beijing? Maybe he would find a job? He could work and study at the same time. Maybe he could send some money back home to support his father? Then maybe his father could work less.

"There!!" His brother started running towards the shrine. They could see the flags now. His father turned his head back to look at him. His father's hazel eyes looked tearful, his face more wrinkled than usual. He wanted to hug his father as if they hadn't seen each other for the longest time. The footfalls increased as his father's image blurred and disappeared. He turned around to his mother. She wasn't there! He could still see familiar faces, but they were no longer in the desert. This cold, gray room was filled with teens he knew from the village. All wearing uniforms. He could recognise them, but they all felt like strangers. He moved his hand to his head only to notice his doppa was missing. The footfalls moved closer and closer and closer. He jolted as someone tapped him on the shoulder. He raised his head to see the face of his teacher: "Speak!"

He leapt out of his seat as the hammer resting on his knees fell to strike the anvil before him:

"I love the Motherland. I love the People. I love the Party. I am Chinese!"

> *Author Note: At the end of the narrative, the protagonist replies, "Ai zuguo, ai renmin, ai dang. Wo shi Zhongguoren." It's a popular PRC slogan that people are forced to say to show loyalty to the Party.*

Wandering

Dilshat Aripov

خوتەن شۇسى

مۇتەللىپ ئىقبال

خوتەن
ئەرلەرگە ۋەتەن
مەلىكسى تاش بۇراندا ئىزنىقىپ يۈرگەن.
يۇتۇپ كەتكەن مەرۋايىتى قۇمنىڭ ئاستىدا
ئىيتماقتا قۇشاق،
ئىيتماقتا ئۆلەڭ.

حۈەنلىكلەر بىرىنى بىر دەيدۇ،
ياڭاق تۈۆىندە مەڭ جىن بار دەيدۇ،
يالغۇز قالار ئىتتىزلىقلار سەھەر ۋە كەچتە
بىر تال گۈلدەك ۋاقىت سولۇپ، ئۆلۈپ كىتىدۇ.

خوتەندە ئادەم يوق،
بىراق
نۇپۇس قانۇننى كۆزگە ئىلماس نۇرغۇن ئاياللار.
مەڭ ئايال
ھەتتا چۆمۈلدەك مىغىلدىغان ئايال،
بالا تۇغۇپ ئۆلۈپ كىتەر ھەتتا چۆشىدە،
يوقتۇر ھىچ ئامال.

خوتەن سۆيۈملۈك شەھەر،
سۆيگۈدەك شەھەر،
كۆكلەپ چىقار مۆھەببىتى توغراق يولىدا.
قۇرۇپ كىتەر سەمىمىيىتى تەنھا ئارالدا،
قالار بۇ شەھەر
دۇنيا ئالدىدا.

خوتەن ئادىمى،
ئەڭ چىڭ ئادەم،
ئەڭ چىن ئادەم.
چۈنكى بۇ خوتەندە
ئۇنىڭدىن باشقا ھىچكىم يوق.
مەن، مەن خوتەن ئادىمى دىگەن.

خوتەن
خەرىتىلەر ئارقىلىق قەشقەرگە تۇتىشىدۇ.
قەشقەر خوتەن ئەمەستۇر،
خوتەن قەشقەر ئەمەستۇر.
بۇندا ئىككى سايە ئۆز-ئارا
بىر-بىرىگە تۇتاشقان بىلەن.

خوتەن ئادىمى
بىر تۆگىنى بوغۇزلىدى.
بۇ تۆگە
قىرىق جان ئىدى.
قىرىق نەۋرە كەلدى قىشىغا،
بۇ شەھەرنىڭ ئىسمى يوق ئىدى،
بۇ شەھەردە ئادەم بار ئىدى.
خوتەن
ئادەملەرگە لىق تولغان شەھەر،
قۇلاق سالار مەسچىت گۈمبىزى
كۆك قەردە ياڭرىسا ئەزان.

خوتەن
ئادەملەرگە لىق تولغان شەھەر.
خوتەن ئادىمى
يەر تىترىيدۇ خۇدانىڭ كۈنى،
ئايغا ئوخشار پۈچۈق كەتمىنى.
ئەمما،
بىرمۇ ئادەم يوق
ئىتىز بىشىدا.

Xoten Accent

Mutellip Iqbal

Xoten
homeland for men
its princess adrift in a stone storm.
Its gems have been lost under the sand
according to the folktales,
according to the songs.

The people of Xoten pronounce one like one,
they say under the walnut trees there are a thousand jinn,
in the morning and nights the farmlands stay empty
time is watered and dies, like a single flower.

There are no people in Xoten,
however
there are thousands of women.
Women swarming like ants
who look down on population laws,
birthing children and dying in their dreams,
there is no other way.

Xoten is a lovely city,
a lovable city,
it sprouts love along poplar roads.
Its friendliness dries up on a solitary island,
this city will be left alone
before the world.

The people of Xoten,
are the strongest,
are the most genuine.
Because in Xoten
there is no one else.
Me, I am a person of Xoten.

Translation | Munawwar Abdulla

Xoten
connects to Qeshqer through maps.
Qeshqer is not Xoten,
Xoten is not Qeshqer.
Although their shadows
connect.

A person from Xoten
slaughtered a camel.
This camel
was forty lives.
Forty grandchildren came to his side,
this city had no name,
this city had people.
Xoten
a city filled with people,
the dome of a mosque listens
when the athaan fills the blue heavens.

Xoten
is a city filled with people.
The people of Xoten
till the land for all of time,
their cracked haddock looks like the moon.
However,
there is no one
at the head of the field.

*We use the Uyghur Latin Yéziqi (ULY) spelling for place
names unless otherwise spelled by the contributor. Xoten
is commonly spelled as Hotan in English, and Qeshqer is
commonly spelled as Kashgar.*

Uyghurs form the fifth largest ethnic group in Kazakhstan and are mostly concentrated in Almaty, as well as smaller Uyghur villages near the border with East Turkistan. Historical migration of Uyghurs from regions now known as East Turkistan to Kazakhstan dates back centuries, but significant migrations occurred during the Russian annexation of the Taranchi Ili Sultanate in 1871 and the establishment of Soviet power in the early 20th century. There was another significant migration of Uyghurs to Kazakhstan in the 1950s and 1960s, following the establishment of the Chinese Communist Party in East Turkistan, forming a basis for differentiation between "yerlik" and recently migrated Uyghurs. While initially being one of the centres of Uyghur political activity during that time, with significant East Turkistan Republic (ETR) members migrating to the region, the collapse of the USSR and Kazakhstan's partnership with China has ceased those activities, although the government does support cultural appreciation and Uyghur schools.

Borders are ever-changing and arbitrary, and this is keenly felt in this region. Border closures during times of political upheaval, as well as changes to language education on either side, has caused separation of communities and families across generations despite living a stone's throw away.

To read further about the identity, language, and history of Uyghurs in Kazakhstan, refer to Ablet Kamalov's paper "Identity of Kazakhstan's Uyghurs: Migration, Homeland, and Language" Central Asian Affairs, 8 (2021) 319-345.

Almaty, Kazakhstan

Dilshat Aripov

 UNDER THE MULBERRY TREE

Aziz's Name

Yadykar Ibraimov

Aziz is now thirty-years-old, and an old friend. I keep thinking about the story he once told me, the story of how he got his name:

My grandmother was not yet thirty when she and my grandfather decided that to continue to stay in Ürümchi was tantamount to death for them, and the only solution was to move to the Soviet Union. At that time they already had three children, two five-year-old daughters – twins, my aunts – and a thirteen-year-old son, my uncle, Aziz.

Grandfather was part of the national army. He had some connections in the Soviet Union; in Kazan he had friends from the Polytechnic Institute, and some of his relatives were in Alma-Ata. As a child I remember always asking my grandmother how she got here, and she would always look somewhere off in the distance and say that she sailed to Alma-Ata on a steamboat. I was surprised and never believed her. How do you come to a landlocked Alma-Ata on a steamboat? But then I found out that there was a real shipping link across the Ili River.

The East Turkistan Republic was nearly destroyed, but bursts of fighting were still ongoing. While waiting for the necessary documents, grandmother stayed with her children in one of the villages near Ghulja. The river port was nearby. One summer day, a package arrived with documents and a letter from grandfather, where he wrote that they should immediately take the first ferry without waiting for him. So they did. Only women and children were on the ferry; even the captain was a young girl in her early twenties. The oldest males were Aziz and a few other twelve-and-thirteen-year-olds.

ئۇجمە دەرىخى ئاستىدا

It was night, tranquil. The summer heat was suffocating. Almost everyone was silent, and those who spoke would only do so in a whisper. Even babies in the arms of their mothers were snuffling quietly; maybe they tried to spread calm to reduce the growing amount of uneasiness on board. The ferry sailed on in the dark. The captain was an excellent mariner, and she felt every curl of the river. Swiftly cutting through the spread-out, burnt steppes, was the stellar canvas of a newborn moon flickering in the silence of the water, framed by the peaks of the great mountains hanging so close in this dark night. The ferry seemed to be standing still while the land passed by.

The captain at the helm was serious, focused, equipped with a skillful gaze. On her slender shoulders, the lives of the entire passenger body. Many of the children gathered around her, observing her every movement with reverent enthusiasm.

Suddenly, breaking the established calm, distant gunshots were heard, and the captain slowed the ship down. Then a boat appeared ahead. The boat peacefully approached the ferry; it was a reconnaissance patrol boat that was supposed to sail continually ahead and give a signal in case of any danger. There should have been two people on the boat, but it stood empty. It slowly sailed past, and behind it, its crew, one by one. Serenity was written on their faces, the sky embraced their bodies. The captain did not move, only her eyelids flinched a little. No one saw, and even she herself did not notice the incredible force with which she squeezed the steering wheel. One of the dead was her sister. There was rustling followed by alarmed whispers from within the ferry. No one was asleep anymore. The situation was clear to all.

Here, on the bridge, they decided to act. There were no extra questions, and there were no long speeches. No tears, no goodbyes, no hugs. And there was no place for doubt. They simply formed into a team. The girl captain and teenage boys. A team of only seven. The captain, opening a rusty iron chest, took out a shabby leather bag. In it, wrapped in a charred blue cloth, was an old hatchet and a dozen daggers, the work of old Yengisar masters. The weapons were alive; it kept the memory of previous fights. She picked up the hatchet; it seemed to glow from the inside, and there was an inscription in Old Uyghur on it. The rest of the weapons were distributed among the young warriors.

The waves of the river softly murmured as the captain moored the boat. The group landed near the rocky shore. In a chain, repeating the movement of the waves, they moved forward, the steel of their daggers gleaming in their hands. There was only one goal ahead. Provide a safe transition. Destroy the enemy. Protect their loved ones. They moved silently, like a pack of young wolves.

Although armed to the teeth, the Chinese soldiers were not ready for a guerrilla attack. Without a sound, a sentry's blood sprinkled the coastal steppe highlands. Up ahead, one could clearly see the silhouettes of unsuspecting soldiers scattered next to a machine gun mounted on a hill, purposed for immigrants.

Meanwhile, a baby cried on the ferry. A young mother lulled him quietly to sleep, singing a strange lullaby.

Ettigendin qarangghuche
Séni kütüp turimen
From dawn to dusk
I will wait for you

From somewhere behind the mountains, crooked feathers of clouds came running, and the gust of a light wind blew a scarf from someone's head. It gently flew along the river.

Menggülük séning
Yüzüngni kömgendek boldum
Forever yours
It's as though I've buried your face

Daggers pitted against the soldiers with swift, cold-blooded movements.

Yengisar is a town near Qeshqer that is renowned for its knives, which range from pocket knives to swords. These handmade Yengisar knives have been celebrated for centuries for their high quality and uniquely ornate handles. Unfortunately, in recent years, the crackdown on knives and Uyghur culture, in general, has decimated the Yengisar knife economy. As a result, the knives purchased by tourists nowadays are typically inauthentic, mass-produced knives made by migrant Chinese workers.

Dutarning avazini tingshighandek boliwatimen
It's as though I am listening to a dutar's melody

Mindless bursts of machine guns lighted distraught faces.

Unutalmaydu, közliringdin aqqan yashlar
They cannot forget, the tears that fell from your eyes

"These are children, these are just children!"

One of the soldiers managed to turn the spotlight in the opposite direction.

Bir kün kelseng méning öyümge
Séni kütüp turimen
If you come to my home someday
I will be waiting for you

At that moment, a darting bullet extinguished the searchlight, but the young warriors had managed to get their share of lead by then, too. Time stopped, time became viscous as honey. Thirteen-year-old Aziz saw one of the Chinese soldiers turning a machine gun towards him. He saw him start shooting; he saw yellow sparks illuminate the soldier's face.

The stunned eyes of the young-faced soldier seemed to be meeting death dutifully. In the same moment a hatchet smashed his forehead and blood sprayed in gusts, ringed with purple flashes. The Chinese lad realised something in this moment, a second before death, as he saw the girl captain; something his mind and soul had never dared to touch. In that second it seemed to him that he was seeing a dance. Once, when he was a first-timer in Uyghur lands, he had seen a similar dance. The movements of this girl with a hatchet in one hand and a dagger in the other made him utterly vulnerable, like nothing before ever had. His mind evoked the sounds of an instrument whose name he could not recall.

It seemed to him that in the midst of whipping blood and firing shots, one of the boys – the one he had just aimed at and shot – picked up this musical instrument and started playing a very strange melody that fascinated him. This was definitely a dance. And the blood lit by sparks was the pattern of her dress.

And these teenagers whirling around showed how beautiful it was; it looked like a picture he had once caught a glimpse of in the city of Turpan.

The girl captain pulled out the hatchet, stopping the dying visions of the young Chinese soldier, then looked around. The Chinese soldiers were destroyed. But not without loss; of the seven, only four stood on their feet.

The bullet managed to pierce the chest of Aziz.

Now I am much older than the man I was named after ever was.

Doppa Series

Sonya Imin

These photographs were taken in the high desert grasslands of the Tohono O'odham people, situated near the US/Mexico border. In some images, the doppa appears as a monument juxtaposed against the vast landscape of the high desert in winter, set upon blocks of concrete or stone and weathered wood. In others, the doppa is nestled in the tall grass, evoking the image of a cradle or overgrown grave. As an Uyghur in exile, this series of photographs presents a visual dialogue from the standpoint of a guest in one desert, while invoking memories and connections to my desert homeland - from the Sonora to the Teklimakan.

The doppa is a traditional hat that has been worn by the Uyghurs and other Central Asian peoples. A doppa is traditionally made of cotton or silk and is usually embroidered with intricate designs. The "gül" pattern shown here features a stylised rose and is a common design worn by Uyghur women. This particular doppa was handmade by women artisans in Uzbekistan as a part of "The Doppi Project" by BENI.

ئۇچمە دەرىخى ئاستىدا

Etles Hoodies

Subi Imam

Many Uyghur homes and private spaces display cultural items, retaining a sense of heritage in foreign lands. Cultural clothing however is often saved for special occasions or performances, if ever worn. The etles hoodie was a way to take a piece of Uyghur culture from our homes into public spaces, adding some of the vibrancy of Uyghur culture to the societies we live in, while also looking good and being comfortable in ethically sourced clothing. Almost 400 of these hoodies were sold, and all of the profits from the hoodies were donated to the Uyghur Mosque and Learning Centre in Canada.

Handmade Traditions

İlminur Efvan

For centuries, centres such as Xoten, Yarkend, Qeshqer, Turpan, Qarasheher, Kucha, Miran, and Ghulja have been recognised as major hubs for the development and production of handcrafted goods. Each of these centres had its own specialty, for instance, Qeshqer was recognised for its proficiency in metalworking, fabric dressing, feltmaking, carpet weaving, production of musical instruments, pottery, and embroidery. Xoten continues to be a highly regarded centre for carpet weaving and sericulture. Yarkend was renowned for its exceptional metalworking, felt products, and carpets.

Art orginally published in The Taste of Uyghur (Teklimakan Uyghur Neshriyati, 2022) by Abduweli Ayup.

Pottery played a significant role in the production of various items such as coating slabs, tiles, household and decorative crockery, lamps, and toys. Common pottery items include amphoras, pitchers, dishes, and bowls. Uyghur potters utilised glaze extensively for coating their dishes, particularly for "chilling vessels" that were used to preserve perishable goods. These vessels were coated with glaze for two-thirds of its height and buried in the ground for the remaining one-third. This was based on the belief that the glaze would prevent the chill from penetrating the vessel. In addition to conventional clay vessels, "sand vessels" which contained a considerable amount of sand can also be found.

Müshük Qiz

Aynur Korla

As an Uyghur in diaspora, I find solace in my cat, whom I call "Qizim". Inspired by my cat and the famous painting of the Girl with a Pearl Earring, I portray my cat as a young Uyghur girl, adorned in golden earrings and a doppa to express our bond through our shared identity. This painting is a tribute to my love for cats, my yearning for family, and my Uyghur heritage.

Tursun

Leena Kuerban

This piece shows traditional elements within Uyghur culture being inspired by my late Grandfather. The piece provokes a sense of nostalgia seeing a veranda covered in the curling vines of grapes which causes me to recollect memories of him.

Conversation with Contributor

LK   *The inspiration for the piece was my grandfather. He could cook every traditional Uyghur dish and he grew many things that you would see back in Turkistan. In my childhood home he had grown an abundance of grapes. They would drape across the carport and fall along the edges, creating a curtain of lush leaves. I would typically see him wearing a knitted vest or sweater; he always looked tidy. I wanted to combine all these elements into a simple illustration so that it would be easily understood.*

I wanted to convey a feeling of nostalgia and longing. I created the piece during my last year of high school because I had missed my grandfather. A period of my life was over and it's hard not to think back to the past about those you've lost.

While developing my work I did numerous sketches and drafts exploring different symbolic elements, layouts, and colour schemes. I purposely chose to focus on three things: the grapes, knitted vest, and doppa. I kept the general shapes bold and simple so that they were easy to view. I limited myself to mainly cooler tones such as blues and purples, as I felt these best portrayed a distant memory.

Missing Home

Ablikim Bughra

Things that remind me of home in a foreign land.

Untitled

Sonya Imin

As a diasporic mixed Uyghur person, I have often felt like my sense of self has been fragmented across time and space. Part of my resilience and resistance against efforts of indigenous erasure is to be in deep relationship to my own Uyghurness, living alongside the complexity of my numerous lived identities.

Isolate

Munawwar Abdulla

I find solace
I say, too late, should I go to the store?
There's no milk left
I expand isotropic-ly

The isotope is like a toxic trope in storybooks
It halves its life to poison others
By no fault of its own
I forgive it, sure
Later, at the end of time, it might remember me
Give me a nod in the right direction

I find solace
True to form
I, so late in the trappings of time
Split each element that feels a little heavy
Attempt to freeze its energy in ice
It expands spherically
Like me, I think
Unbound by half-lives I am at the store
Drinking a carton of milk

If the ice melts into spring
Who will be there to remember it?
The storybooks, I think
They can point us in the right direction

Time springs forth one unit of decay
May the witnesses write that down
I sit gently in a moment
A pocket of oblivion
I find solace
I find solace

Khoshang

Ayesha Erkin

I've learned that food is political.

I continually wrestle with being a mixed diaspora immigrant wanting to build a new, rooted life, but simultaneously feeling a heightened sense of responsibility to use my freedom for those that are not free.

I'm alive. So, I speak.

I'll never be able to 100% claim a country, but I can say I am of the greater diaspora of my countries — East Turkistan having a heavy influence on my upbringing.

Preserving culture through the lens of food and memory is my way of making others aware of the ongoing genocide in East Turkistan. So, let's introduce Khoshang.

Uyghur cuisine has several types of pocket foods (i.e. dumplings) but this one is the most extra dumpling I've had the honour of devouring for the entirety of my life. Uyghur pockets are an art form in themselves. For khoshang, you have to wrestle with using the perfect amounts of meat and dough, while simultaneously twisting the top into a happy little spiral. Then you proceed to deep fry them to a deliciously crispy brown colour and then lay them in a steamer to expand and soften.

As with almost every Uyghur cuisine in our household, this is served with laza (chili oil) and sirka (vinegar). It's pretty unique in the dumpling family - a perfect example of the uniqueness of Uyghur culture.

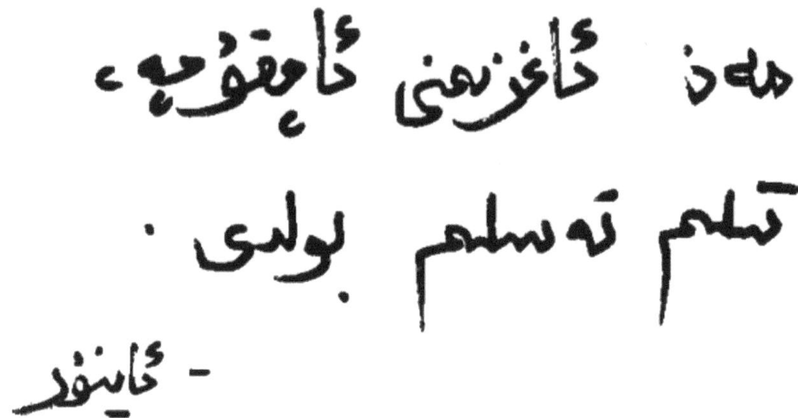

By the time I opened my mouth,
  my tongue had already surrendered.

- Aynur

Translation | Joshua L. Freeman

Conversation with Contributor

AK   *The political environment, including people's apathy towards the Uyghurs and the complexity of our crisis, makes me feel small and helpless. I want the world to know how hard it is to convey messages and raise our voices. I wish they knew how difficult and frustrating it is for me to raise my voice.*

Calligraphy

İlminur Efvan

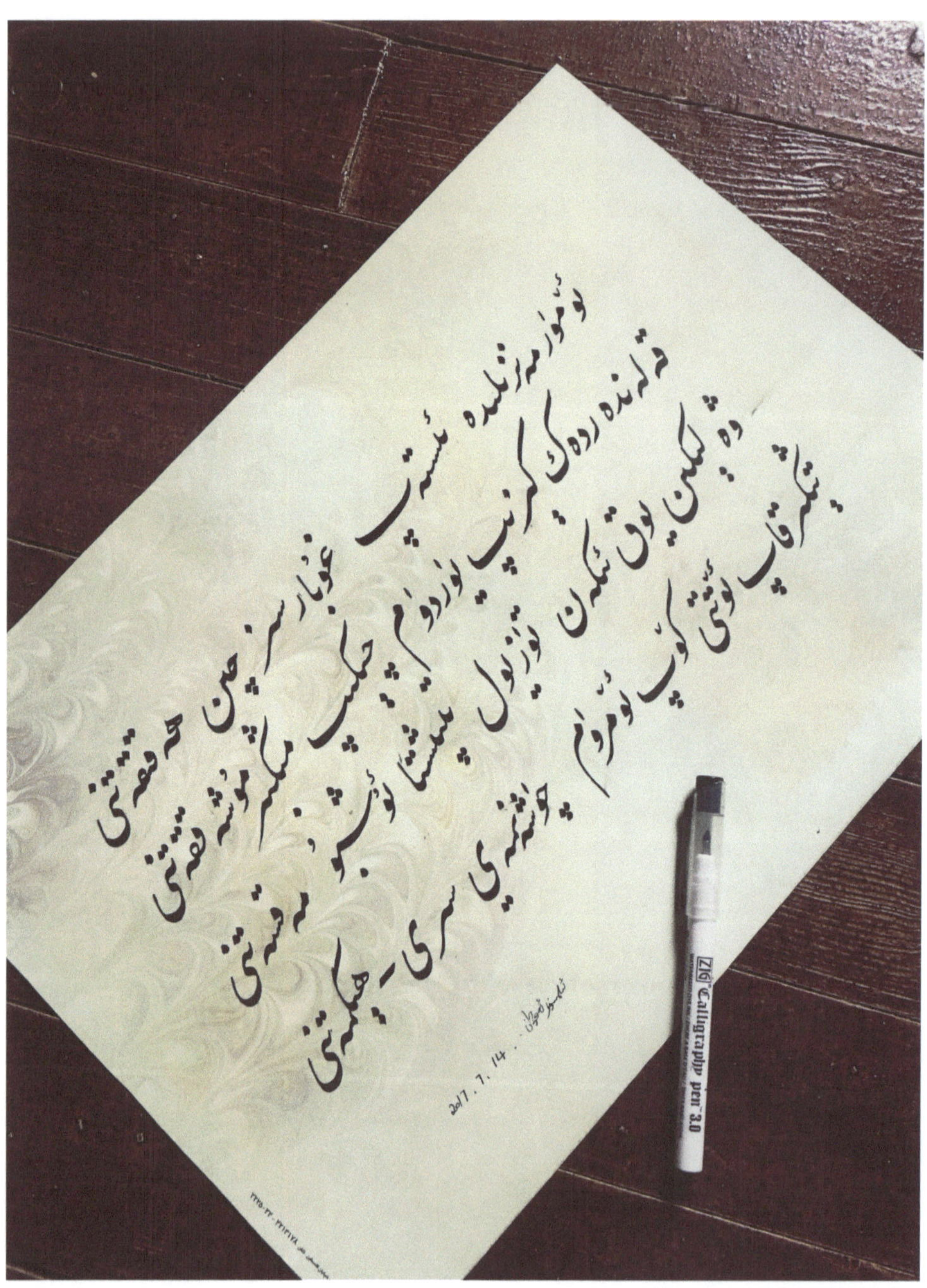

ئۆمۇر مەنزىلىدە ئىستەپ غۇبارسىز چىن ھەقىقەتنى
قەلەندەردەك كېزىپ يۈردۈم چېكىپ مىڭبىر مۇشەققەتنى
ۋە لېكىن يوق ئىكەن توز يول تېپىشقا ئۇشبۇ مەقسەتنى
تېڭىرقاپ ئۆتتى كۆپ ئۆمرۈم چۈشەنمەي سىرى-ھېكمەتنى

Ömür menzilide istep ghubarsiz chin heqiqetni
Qelenderdek kézip yürdüm chékip mingbir musheqqetni
We lékin yoq ıken tüz yol tépishqa ushbu meqsetni
Téngirqap ötti köp ömrüm chüshenmey siri-hékmetni

*Uyghur calligraphy is a unique form of Perso-Arabic calligraphic script that has
continued to develop since it was adopted after Islam was introduced around the 10th
century. There are twelve main forms of Uyghur calligraphy, each differing markedly
from one another. Uyghur calligraphy has been a well-respected and widely-visible
practice for centuries, and one of the main conduits through which knowledge of our
society had been passed down throughout eras, especially from Chaghatay script.
In the diaspora there are a few practitioners concentrated in Türkiye or Central Asia,
and efforts to pass on the knowledge to the next generation are also happening in the
United States.*

بارالمىدىم
لېكىن ئۈنتۆمدىم
بېرىشقا ئامالسىز قالدىم
ئۈنتۈشقا راۋاسىز.

ئاھلىرىم كەتتى نە-نەلەرگە
سۆكۈتمگىدىن بۆلەك كەلمىدى سەندىن بىر شەپە.

ئەي ئانا ۋەتىنىم
بۇ تاپتا تىرىشۋاتىمەن سېنىڭ سۆكۈتمگىنى چۈشەنمەككە.

بەلكىم
مېنى «ۋىجدانسىز» دەۋاتىمسەن ئىچىڭدە
«ئۆزىنى سۆيگەندەك سۆيمىدى» دەپ پەرياد قىلىۋاتىمسەن
يۈرىكىڭدە
«قايتىپ كېلمەن دەپ مەندىن بىرەر ئوچۇممۇ ئېلىپ
كەتمىگەن ئىدىكغۇ،
قەدرىمنى بېڭى يەرلەر ئۈنتۈلدۈردىمۇ؟»
دەپ مەندىن سوئال سوراۋاتىمسەن شۇ سۆكۈتمگىدە.

ئەي ئانا ۋەتىنىم
مەن «ۋىجدانسىز» ئەمەس
چارىسىزمەن
ساڭا قايتىش غەملىرى ئىچىدە ياشاۋاتقان يالغان غەمسىزمەن.
«ۋەتەن» دەپ ئېيتىلغان ناخشىلارنىڭ تېكستىدىن
تەسىرلىنىدىغان بىر بىچارىمەن.

بىلەمسەن
سېنىڭ بىر ئوچۇمىڭنى
ياق
بىر چىمدىمىڭنىمۇ ئېلىپ كېتىشتىن شۇنچە تەستە باسقان
ئىدىم ئۆزۈمنى
چۈنكى
قورققان ئىدىم
شۇ سەن بىلەن پۈراپ تۇرسام ھىدىكغنى
شۇ ۋەجىدىن
سېنى بىرىپ كۆرۈشتىن بەلكىم توختىتىۋالار پۇتلىرىم مېنى

بارالمىغىنىم ئۈنتۆغىنىم ئەمەس

زۆھرە ئۇيغۇر

بارالمىغىنىم ئۆنتۈغىنىم ئەمەس
سۆيمىگىنىم ئەمەس
چۈنكى سەن ئوبدان بىلىسەن
سۆيگۈمنىڭ مۆتلەق ياكى بەلكىلىكىنى
ئۆگىنىشمدا ۋە ياكى يۈرۈكۈمدىلىكىنى.

مەن سىنى سۆيىمەن
سەن مەن ئۈچۈن
«ئەڭ ئىسىل كۈي»
«ئەڭ چىرايلىق يىزىلغان قۇر»
سۆيۈشكە ئۆمرۈم يەتمەس بىر ئۆلۈغ مۇھەببەت.

بىلمەن ئەي ۋەتىنىم
شۇ سۆكۈتلىرىڭ ئىچىدە سەنمۇ مىنى سىغىنداڭ شۇنچە
چۈنكى
چۈشلىرىمدە ئايان بولغىنىڭدا مىنى كۆرۈپ
قىزارغان ئىدى كۆزلىرىڭ
تاتارغان ئىدى يۈزلۈرىڭ
قىپىدىن چىقاي دېگەن ئىدى يۈرىكىڭ
ئىچىشقان ئىدى، دىماغلىرىڭ
مىنى پەپلىمەككە تەمشەلگەن ئىدى قوللىرىڭ
مىنى ھەددىدىن زىيادە سىغىنغىنىڭ ئۈچۈن شۇنچە ئاچچىق
ئىدى سۆزلىرىڭ.
مەن ئۈچۈن بۇلار
بۇلارنىڭ ھەممىسى مۇھەببەت، لىققىدە مۇھەببەت.

ئەي ئانا ۋەتىنىم
يىراقلاردا سىنى سىغىنغان ھىسلىرىم
بەلكى سىنى قايتا كۆرەلمەس چۈشلىرىم
مەيلى ئەمەسمۇ
چۈنكى
مەن ئۈچۈن
يىراقتا تۇرۇپ سىنى سۆيەلىشىممۇ بىر بەخت ئەمەسمۇ؟

Diasporic Dilemma

Kabir Qurban

"Where are you from?" I was asked at a very young age. I wondered, "Well, I was born in Kazakhstan, I speak Farsi, but I know I am Uyghur." I understood that I was Uyghur, but I didn't know what being Uyghur meant. Having visited my homeland multiple times as a kid, I almost believed I had a sovereign nation.

So to him I said I'm from Uyghurstan.

"Which yoghurt stand?" he asked.

At that point I knew I had to learn more about myself, so I went home. I asked my grandma, "What is it that I am?" and she said, "Your Grandfather used to trade almonds." I asked my mother, "Who am I?" and she said, "Your Grandfather was a goldsmith in East Turkistan." My initial understanding of my roots was never a sense of victimhood.

Having visited my homeland for the last time in 2009, I witnessed the upheaval that took place after the Ürümchi massacre. Seeing a tank on the road I smiled at my mum, and I said, "Hey Apa look! It's a tank." I've never seen her slap a smile off my face so quickly. That night I called home telling my dad, "I'm so excited to have seen a tank today Dada." Once again she hit me. If I only knew that she wasn't trying to hurt me, but rather she was trying to make me aware of the hurt that had already been inflicted on us. Now I reminisce the times I was able to walk freely on my own land which I no longer belong to. I remember going to protests and fighting for my "freedom", but I lived a privileged life and had trouble understanding what freedoms I'd been deprived of.

In 2016, I was merely a high school student on my journey towards success. Then the news hit. At first, I thought I only lost touch with my uncle, with whom my bond wasn't as deep as it was for my mother. I can only imagine the anguish that every Uyghur family member holds around the world. Yet, we still fight to this day, never giving up and never giving up hope.

So they asked me again, "Where are you from?"

I say East Turkistan, although the language of my people doesn't flow effortlessly on my tongue; I will never stop speaking.

The diasporic dilemma is one that understands the anguish of a missing homeland, to one I have not been accustomed to. Having only smells, cuisines and clothing to remember my land by. We were not always victims; we are scholars, poets, musicians, aristocrats, tradesmen, engineers, doctors, lawyers, pharmacists, and we are proud. Our culture is rich, almost 4000 years old. Yes, my identity has gained a sense of victimhood, but I won't let this hyphenated identity water down my ambition. I am still a man, proud of my identity. Even though I am bridging my identity to my roots, I am thankful for the diasporic experience for I am able to fuel my journey of filling in the gaps between my apparent identity, and my ethnic dilemma.

Conversation with Contributor

KQ *I always think of the time when I initially started to unpack my survivor's guilt. I was camping in the Pacific Northwest, in the most beautiful scenery, wondering how I could allow myself to enjoy moments as such when I have family missing.*

Muqam

Dilshat Aripov

Uyghur Muqam is a traditional musical and oral narrative art form characterised by its use of elaborate melodies and rhythms, sung lyrics, and musical instruments such as the dutar, rawap (shown here), and satar. Performed for cultural and social events, Muqam is a central part of Uyghur cultural heritage. Currently, there are elements of the Muqam that have been removed or modified by the Chinese state, including references to Islam or to the motherland. These sanitised versions are often shown as stage performances for tourists or as propaganda in state media.

Visits

Munawwar Abdulla

The moon disappears for three days

moma visits me in dreams
old photos do her no justice
lying in a hospital gown
fading into the night

she wields knowledge like a brush
poised, prepared, precise like the dots
on the wax acupuncture figures she kept,
refreshing her medical fingers

a symphony of older conversations
her laugh and scathing comments

I had forgotten, as the moon waned
her charisma and clarion voice
so different to mine

but she would whisper at times, so
I learnt our calligraphy
how to draw trees

colouring my mind as her memories fade
speaking to me as she spoke to bowa
years ago, during days of labour
smiling vibrant as the full moon

Swallow

Jangul Baurjan

My ata, in spite of my age, calls me 'kulnym' (my foal),
he laughs when I ask why we have no ancestors buried in this country,
where kids make fun of my name
and shame my poor apa's veil.
'janym menym (soul of mine),
our home is
wherever in the shadow of our mountains.'

back then I took everything for granted.
even now, so many years have silently passed
and I'm still learning from your words:
how profound the depth of your yearning,
of your generosity (boundlessness) to love before (despite) loss.

for those like us, who have to utter half-truths,
for whom absence is like the sky,
I wish in my next life, or at least in my dreams,
I can be born again as the autumn swallow,
whose offspring returns every spring,
and build nests from rubble onto concrete.
in another life, I want to meet my apa ata again,
and tell them,
one day we will no longer be envious of the birds.
until then, my refuge,
my home is
wherever so long as in your shadow.

Apa ata here means grandparents.

Grandparents play a central role in our families, and their homes are often referred to as the "chong öy", which literally means "big house", or main house, where everyone gathers during important occasions. At times, they take on the role of parents, especially if the biological parents are young, or absent due to a variety of reasons. As a result, some children may refer to their grandmothers as "apa" and their mothers as sisters.

Dreams

Abdushukur Muhammet

If I went to the plaza
with my dream, yellowed like a ripened apricot
in the tamarisk basket left by my mother
will it resemble a passer-by on the street?

One face
of the street corner is filled with blood red apples.
Perhaps they'd fallen from the setting sun.

Sometimes dreams
embrace me with their coarse arms, like apricot branches.
I know
the blood of time drips in my breast over the years,
like a barefoot boy picking ears of wheat,
ripping his heels.

The self doesn't have seasons.
From simply the scent of withered memories,
I fall suddenly into a dream,
the way a stone falls on a quiet lake.

The rings that ripple from my dream
take me to an even farther night.

27 May 2021

Translation | Munawwar Abdulla

جوش

ئابدۇشۇكۇر مۇھەممەت

كىشمىش ئۆزۈككتەك سارغىيىپ پىشقان چوشۈمنى
ئانامدىن قالغان يۇلغۇن سىۋۆتتە
ئېلىپ چىقسام رەستىگە
ئوخشاپ قالارمۇ كوچىدا يۈرگەن بىرسىگە؟

كوچا دوقمۇشى
بىر يۈزى قاندەك قىزارغان ئالمىغا تولغان
بەلكىم ئۇ پىتمۇاتقان قۇياشتىن چۇشۇپ قالغان.

بەزىدە چوش
ئۆزۈك شىخىدەك يىرىك بىلىكى بىلەن قوچاقلار مېنى
بىلمەن
يىللاردىن بۇيان باغرىمدا ئاقماقتا ۋاقىتنىڭ قېنى
خۇددى يالاڭئاياغ باشاق تەرگەن بالىدەك
يىرتىلىپ تاپىنى.

ئۆزۈمنىڭ پەسلى يوق
پەقەت غازاڭ بولغان ئەسلىمىنىڭ پۇراقلىرىدىن
خۇددى جىمجىت كۆلگە تاش چۇشكەندەك
تۇيۇقسىز چۇشىمەن چوشنىڭ ئىچىگە
چۇشۈمىدىن تارىغان قاتمۇ قات چەمبەر
ئېلىپ بارار مېنى تېخىمۇ يىراق كېچىگە.

2021-يىلى 27-ماي

I Dream My Friends' Faces

Mirshad Ghalip

I see my friends in my dreams at night,
perhaps I just miss them, perhaps it's a sign.
The windy city's gusts cannot reach Korla,
the greetings I send remain unheard.

The past looks at me with a haughty laugh,
I don't understand where the future has gone.
Each night I sink into my dreams,
like a bike with a wobbly wheel sinks into mud.

A face wrinkled by the lines of laughter,
soccer games in the street without a ball,
a curly-haired guy grinning in the cold,
the fire station shouting in our young ears—
our only meeting place is in my dreams.
And I curse the morning that pulls me from them.

10 August 2020
Chicago

Conversation with Contributor

MG   *The fact that I missed them drove me to write. I posted it where my friends could see it. I believe they saw it and understood... I cannot mention their names because the police may look for them if they think they have contacts in other countries.*

Translation | Joshua L. Freeman

چۈشۈمدە ئاغىنىلىرىم بىلەن دىدار

سىرشات غالىپ

چۈشلىرىمدە كۆرىمەن ئاغىنىلىرىمنى
سىغىنىشىمدۇ ياكى بىشارەتمىدۇ.
شامال شەھەرىدكى شامال كورلىغا بارماسمىش
سالىممىنى ئىبىتاي دېسەم ئالماسمىش.

ئۆتمۈش ماڭا قاراپ كۆرەڭلەپ كۈلىدۇ
كەلگۈسىننىڭ نەلەرگە كەتكەنلىكنى بىلمەيمەن.
چۈشۈمگە پېتىپ كېتىمەن ھەر ئاخشام،
خۇددى چاقى كالاڭ كەتكەن ۋېلسىپىت لايغا پاتقاندەك.

تولا كۆلۈپ قورۇق چۈشكەن چىراي،
كوچىدا پۇتبول يوق تۆرۈپ ماغسېپىچە چۆگلەش،
قەھرىتاندا ھىنجىيىپ قالغان بۆدۈرە ساچ،
كىچىكىمىزدە قۇلاقلىرىمىزغا ۋاقىرشىپ ئۈينىغان
ئوت ئۆچۈرۈش ئىدارىسى،
دىدارى پەقەت چۈشۈمدىلام.
شۇڭا مېنى تارتىپ چىققان سەھەرگە نەپرىتىم كېلەر.

2020-يىلى 10-ئاۋغۇست
چىكاگو

ئاپتور بىلەن سۆھبەت

م.غ سېغىنىشىم مېنى قەلەم تەۋرەتكۈزدى. دوستلىرىم كۆرەلەيدىغان ئىجتىمائىي تاراتقۇغا چىقاردىم. ئۇلار كۆرۈپ چۈشەندى دەپ ئويلايمەن...گەرچە شېئىرىمدىكى ھېسسىياتنى چۈشىنىش مۇمكىن بولسىمۇ، مەن كەملەرنى تەسۆرلەۋاتقىنىمنى شۇ دوستلىرىمدىن باشقىلار چۈشەنمەيدۇ. چۈنكى ئۇلارنىڭ ئىسمىنى ئاتىسام بولمايدۇ. چەت ئەل بىلەن ئالاقىسى باركەن دەپ ئۇلارنى ساقچىلار ئىزدىشى مۇمكىن.

UNDER THE MULBERRY TREE

Memory Structure

Camilla Dilshat

Installation
Found branches, latex, jute twine, red thread, pink thread, grey unknown
string, copper wire, found aggregate concrete, unfired buff clay, unglazed
ceramics (terracotta and buff), elastic bands, salt dough, acrylic.

My tongues are reaching out to distant memories, touching, licking, feeling.
Piecing pieces back together but they are overlapping and floating in an
empty space, a skeleton shelter. I feel my skin stretch and pucker, then relax,
letting patterns imprint onto it. The smell of baking naan in plastic bags and
cooked stripped chicken bones waft through the space. I hear the stretch
and smack of noodles merging into snakes sliding down the branches. My
tongue gets wrapped… Or am I just slurping? I stick out my tongue again, is
it hot? Have I got something stuck on it? Just brittle bones and rickety chairs
to squat on. I sit down and I braid my hair until my arms are burning. Then it
fades.

Conversation with Contributor

CD   *"Memory Structure" is a sculptural installation piece depicting the skeleton of a shelter constructed out of found branches. Within the shelter, what I call "memory objects" inhabit and float through the space, reference fleeting memories and senses from weten.*

At the beginning, this process acted as a therapeutic venture towards preserving memories. I previously lost all the photos I took when I was in weten due to accidentally wiping my phone. I then began reflecting on the ephemeral nature of memories. As time passed I felt my memories become more distant as if they were a story and I wanted to act against this. I began engaging in sculpture making to infuse these created objects with a memory I desired to capture. Throughout the process, what I found was a struggle to remember specific details. What was the exact shape of that naan I ate?

I realised that my memories began merging together and overlapping. Instead of specific, tangible objects, what emerged were fragmented ones. I realised that the power in remembrance did not lay in specifically remembering exactly how something looked, but instead, of faint senses, feelings, and muscle memory: sweating naan in plastic bags, noodles wrapping around your tongue or rolling out snake-y dough. Therefore, I allowed the fragmented objects to exist as they are, a skeletal qapaq, severed tongues, and a pile of brittle clay bones. They had power in their fragmented form, their sensory associations elevated and filled with symbolism.

I hope people feel the power contained within the piece — they feel that the objects are important, like objects placed in a shrine. That they reference specific experiences of touch, taste, and feeling even though the viewers won't necessarily have access to the knowledge of my personal memories. Very specific memories. Finding a bug randomly in your mouth that somehow made it onto your tongue. Slurping noodles. Squatting. Creating a pile of chicken bones. Walking past hanging fabric. Heat.

A Special Place

Sarah Suzuk

I CAN SEE MOUNTAIN RANGES THAT GO ON AND ON...

I CAN SMELL THE RAIN ON A COOL SUMMER'S NIGHT.

I CAN TASTE THE NAAN FROM THAT BAKERY DOWN THE STREET.

IT MIGHT STILL BE THERE,

IN SOME SHAPE OR FORM.

BUT IT'S GONE FOREVER.

كامېرا

سەردار ئەھەتئېلى

ھەممىنى ئەڭ سەممىي رەۋىشتە خاتىرىلەيدىغان ۋاقىت بولغاندى. تاڭنۇر بىلەن كۆرۈشكىسەم كىيەرمەن دەپ يۈيۈپ قويغان ئاق كالتە ئىشتىنىمنى ئالماشتۇرۇپ، ئۈستۈمگە ئۈچ يىل ئاۋۋالقى تۇغۇلغان كۈنۈمدە ئېرىشكەن ئەتىرنى سېپىپ ۋە چىچىمنى ئاشۇ كۈندىكىدەك تاراپ، بىر كامېرا سېتىۋېلىش ئۈچۈن يولغا چىقتىم. سىرتتا ياز باشلىناي دېگەندى. سەھەردىكى ئۇچۇق نەرسىلەردىن ھاۋا، ئەتى بار قوشنىمىزنىڭ ئىشىكى ۋە تاماق كۆتۈرۈپ ماڭغۇچىنىڭ يوپكىسىنىڭ رەڭگى بار ئىدى. تۈتۈق نەرسىلەر بولسا، يول بويىدىكى باققالنىڭ چىرايى، جىگىننىڭ ئىشكالىسى ۋە ئۈننىڭ نامەلۇم خىيالى ئىدى.

«ئاللا مېنى كۆرۈپ تۇرىدۇ»، «رازىيە جالاپ»، «ئادەم بولسىڭىز بۇ يەرگە...» دېگەن خەتلەر قالايمىقان يېزىلغان تامنىڭ تۆۋىدە ئۈچ كىچىك بالا ئويناۋاتاتتى. نېمىشقىكەن، ماڭا ھەممە كىچىك بالا مەستتەكلا كۆرۈنەتتى ھەم ھەر قېتىم مەست بولۇپ قالغىنىمدا، ئۆزۈمدىن دائىم شۇنداق سورايتتىم: كىچىك ۋاقتىمدا دەل مۇشۇنداق ھالەتتىمىدىم؟ بېشىم قىزىغان، قۇلىقىم پاڭ، ئېغىزىم يېرىم ئېچىلغان، دىققىتىم بىر نۇقتىغا شۇنچىلىك مەركەزلەشكەن، ئەتراپىم بولسا غۇۋۇۋا. باللىقتىكى بارلىق رەسىملىرىمدە، مەگزىم ئاپتاپتىكى بايراقتەك قىزارغان، كۆزلىرىم كېچىدىكى بايراقتەك خۇمارلىق ھالدا، ئاپپاراتقا گويا بىر چوش كۆرۈۋاتقان ئادەمدەك قاراپ تۇرار ئىدىم.

شاماللار تېنىمنى يېنىك ئەندىكتۈرەتتى. ئۇخشاش فورمىلارنى كىيىشكەن ئوقۇغۇچىلار ئالدىمدىن چوغۇلدەك كېلىشەتتى. تونۇرلاردىن قومۇرۇلىۋاتقان نان ۋە كاۋاپ پۇراقلىرى ئارقمىدىن خېلى يەرگىچە ئەگىشەتتى. دوقمۇش— دوقمۇشتا تەكشۇرۇلۇشنى كۈتۈپ، قولىنى كەڭ ئىچىپ تۇرغان ۋە زوڭزىيىپ ئولتۇرۇپ ھەجىيىۋاتقان ياشلار، ئېغىز ئورۇندۇقتا ئولتۇرۇپ، دوغىنى ئاسمانغا ئېغىز ئېتىۋاتقان ئاياللار، باغچىغا ئارقىسىنى قىلىپ ئولتۇرۇپ، بېغىزىنى ماكچايغان كەشلەرگە زەردە بىلەن تىقىۋاتقان موزدۇزلار ۋە ئۇلارنىڭ ئالدىدىكى يەنە بىر پاي كەشنى تۈتقىنىنچە يالاڭ ئاياق ئولتۇرغان چوكانلار، يالىلغۇچىنىڭ كېلىشنى ساقلاپ، قىمار ئوينىاپ ئولتۇرۇشقان توپ—توپ مەدكارلار، قاچىلىرىنى يولدىن ئۆتكەن ھەر بىر ئادەمگە تەڭلەپ ئولتۇرغان قېتىقچىلار، شەپكەسنى قولىدا چۆرگىلەتىپ، مۇسادىرە قىلىنغان توكسكىلمىت ئۈستىدە ئولتۇرۇپ، كىراكەشنىڭ تەلمۈرۇشلىرىگە پىسەنت قىلمايۋاتقان شەھەر باشقۇرۇش خادىملىرى، بېكەتلەردىكى خالىس ئورۇندۇقتا ئولتۇرۇپ، ئىشقا كىچىكىپ قىلىشتىن ئەنسىرەۋاتقان خىزمەتچىلەر، ئاغزىدا گۆھەر چىشلەۋالغان تاش

شەرنىڭ يېنىدا ئولتۇرۇپ ئۆزىنى يالۋاتقان مۇشۇكلەر كۆز ئالدىمدىن بىر-بىرلەپ ئۆتۈشكە باشلىدى. يېشىل دەرەخ ئاستىدىكى يېشىل قىسىملار قىزىل چىراغ ئاستىدىكى قىزىل پىكاپلارغا شۇبھىلىك نەزەر تاشلايتتى.

بىر ساترىياشخانىغا كىردىم، ئۇدۇلۇمدا ئولتۇرغان بىرىننىڭ پۇتىنى ئۆزۈمنىڭكى دەپ قىلىپ چۆچۈپ كەتتىم. بىر ئاشخانىغا كىردىم، تامدىكى رۇبائىي ماڭا شۇكۇر قىلىش ھەققىدە نەسىھەت قىلدى. بىر بانكىغا كىردىم، مۇلازىمەت ماشىنىسى مېنىڭ خەنجە تەلەپپۇزۈمنى دۇراپ سۆزلىدى. ماگىزىنلارنىڭ ئەينەك ئىشىكىدىن بىر ئەرۋاھتەك، سەي بازىرىدىن بىر قەرزداردەك، كىتابخانا ئالدىدىن بىر ئەسلىمىدەك ئۆتتۈم.

كۆزلىرىنى قىسقان، چەكچەيگەن، ھىجايىغان، ھەيران قالغان، ئاچچىقلانغان، ھۆرپەيگەن، دومسايغان، خۇدىنى بىلمىگەن، يىغلىغان ھەرخىل ماشىنىلار يوللاردىن ئۆتۈۋشەتتى. گەرچە قاراشلىرى ئوخشىمىسىمۇ، ئۇلارنىڭ ھەر بىرىنىڭ بىر ئادەمگە بولغان ئىشتىھاسى ئوخشاش ئىدى. ماشىنا ئاۋازلىرى قۇلقىمغا گويا دېڭىز شاۋقۇنىدەك بېسىپ كىرىپ، بىر قۇلۇلە قېپىمدا ياڭرىغاندەك ئۆزۈن ياڭرايتتى.

سائەت ئون ئىككى يېرىم بولغاندا، قولۇمدىكى سۇ يېرىم بولغاندا، كۆڭلۈم تېخىمۇ يېرىم بولغاندا، ئۆزۈمنى «نۇر ھايات» دوختۇرخانىسىنىڭ ئاستىدا، كامىراننىڭ سۇرىتى ئاستىدا بايقىدىم:

‏– ھە سولامبەر، نېمە بۇ يەرلەردە يۈرۈيسەن؟ – دەۋاتاتتى ئۇ، خالتىسىدىكى نەشپۇتلىرى بىلەن ماڭا تەڭ ھىجىيىپ.

‏– شەھەرنىڭ پۇتكۈل بۇلۇڭ-پۇچقاقلىرىغا ئوخشاش – دېدىم مەن ئۇنىڭغا، – ئۆيۈمدىمۇ بىر كامېرا بولۇشى كېرەك. قىزىق يېرى، بۇ نەرسىنى ساتىدىغان ماگىزىنلار يوقنىڭ ئورنىدا ئىكەن.

‏– سەن جايىنى تاپالمىغان گەپ. – شۇنداق دەۋېتىپ، تاماكا قېپىدىن ئىككى تال تاماكا چىقاردى ۋە بىرىنى ماڭا تەڭلىدى. – مەن بىر يەرنى بىلمەن.

ئۇ كۆپ نەرسىلەرنى بىلەتتى، سودا-سېتىققا ماھىر ئىدى. ئۇنىڭ ئۈستىگە، ھامان بىر كۆنى پۇتكۈل ئىشلارنى تاشلاپ، زېھنىنى كىنوچىلىققا ئاتىۋېتىشنى ئۇيلايتتى.

چاقماق بىلەن ئوت تۇتاشتۇرۇردى، ئۆزۈن شۇراپ پۇۋلىدۇق. بۇ پەسىلدە ئۇزۇلۇكسىز ياغىدىغان توپا، سودا كاساتلىقى ۋە چۈشتە نېمە يېگەنلىكمىز توغرىسىدا پاراڭلاشتۇق. مەن چېكىپ بولغان تاماكنى يول ياقىسىدىكى گۈللۈككە ئاتتىم. كامران يەرگە «شالاقىدە» بىرنى تۆكۈرۈپ دەسسىدى-دە، ماڭا ھازىرقى تېخىمۇ جىددىي ۋە مۇھىم ئىشنىڭ بۇ بىر كېلۇ كورلا نەشپۇتى بىلەن 723-نومۇرلۇق

كېسەلخانىدىكى مۆئەللىمىمنى يوقلاش ئىكەنلىكىنى، ئاندىن كېيىن ماڭا كامېرا ئېلىشىپ بېرەلەيدىغانلىقىنى ئېيتتى. ماقۇل بولدۇم.

دەرۋازىۋەن بىزگە «نىمە مەقستىڭلار بار؟» دەۋاتقاندەك سەپ سالدى. بىز بارىدىغان بىنا بىنالارنىڭ ئەڭ ئىچكىرىسىدە ئىدى.

– دوختۇرخانىلارنىڭ لىپتى غەلىتە–ھە؟

– تار، ئۈزۈن، مەينەت، سېسىق، مەخسۇس جەسەتلا يۆتكەيدىغاندەك، داتلاشقان، خۇنۇك، ئىغىر، ئاستا، بۈزۈق، جاھىل.

ھايال بولمايلا كېسەلخانىنى تاپتۇق. مۆئەللىم بىر قولدا تېلېفون بىر قولدا كارۋاتتىكى ئايالنىڭ قولىنى تۇتۇپ ئولتۇرغانىكەن، بىزنى كۆرۈپ ئورنىدىن تۇردى، قىزغىن سالاملاشتۇق. ئۇنىڭ ئۈچىنجى بالىسى تۇغۇلغانىدى. تامدىكى تېلېۋىزوردا بىر مەيدان مۇسابىقە بېرىلىۋاتاتتى. نەتىجە ئىككىمدە بىر ئىدى. كامران ئۆخلاۋاتقان بوۋاقنى ئەركىلىتىشتىن ۋاز كېچىپ، ئۇنى «بەك ئوماق تۇغۇلۇپتۇ» دەپ ماختىدى.

– ئەتتۆۋارلانماي قويۇۋلغان ئىسىم، ئۈنتۇلۇپ كەتسەمۇ رەنجىمەگۈلۈك–تە، – دېدى، يەنە بىر قېتىم دادا بولغۇچى. ئىنىقكى، ئۇ بالىغا قانداق ئىسىم قويۇش ھەققىدە كۆپ ئويلانغانىدى. – بىراق ئۆزگىچە ئىسىملارنى ئويلاپ تاپماق تەسكەن، ئۇنىڭ ئۈستىگە بەك ئالاھىدە بولۇپ كەتسە، تەزىمغا ئالدۇرۇشمۇ بىر مەسىلە ئىكەن.

قارشى تەرەپنىڭ ھۇجۇمچىسى چەكلەنگەن رايون ئىچىدە يالغان يىقىلدى. رىپېر ئىپياده بىلدۇرمىدى. ئىكراندا ھۇجۇمچىنىڭ پورلەشكەن ئىپتەك مۇسكۇللىرىغا ئالاھىدە كۆزۈنۈش بېرىلدى. 1990-يىللاردا، مانچېستېرنىڭ بىر داڭلىق ھۇجۇمچىسى بار ئىدى. ئاڭلاشلارغا قارىغاندا، ئەگەر مۇسابىقە باشلىنىپ ئۇ بىتەرەپ قالغان تۈنجى توپ مۇۋەپپەقىيەتلىك بولمىسا، ئۇنىڭ ئىپادىسى پۈتۈن مەيدان ناچار بولارمىش. تەلەي، ئال، ماھارەت قاتارلىقلارنىڭ بىرىمۇ ئۇنىڭغا كۆلۈپ باقمايدىكەنتۇق.

– شۇنداق، بالىنى بەرگەن خۇدايىم رىزقىنىمۇ قوشۇپ بېرىدۇ. ئەجبا ئىنگمىز ئۆزى ياراتقان نەرسىنى ئۆزى خارلىقتا قويارمۇ؟!

– ئىككى تەرەپنىڭ ئوتتۇرا مەيدانىدكى تىركىشىشى كەسكىنلەشمەكتە. – دېدى چۈشەندۈرگۈچى.

نۇرغۇن يىللار ئىلگىرى، مېنىڭ پۇتبول مەكتىپىگە كىپتۇۋاتقىنىمنى ئاڭلىغان تاكسى شوپۇرى ئارقىسىغا ئۆرۈلگىنىچە ماڭا قاراپ: «ئاناڭ بولسىمۇ دەۋرەي ما گەپنى، پۇتبول دېگەن باغۇ ئۇكام، قارشى تەرەپنىڭ ئانىسىنى سكمە دەپ تۇرۇپ

ئوينايدىغان ئۇيۇن» دېگەندى، ئۇتتۇرا بارمىقىنى شىددەت بىلەن چىقىرىپ. لېكىن نېمىشقىكىن، ھەر قېتىم مۇشۇ ئىش ئېسىمگە كەلسلا، «ئاۋۇ ماريا» دېگەن ناخشا قۇلاق تۈۋۈمدە جاراڭلايتتى.

— ياقەي، مەكتەپكە بەرمەي بولامدۇ؟! شۇنداقتىمۇ بىرىنچىسى يەنىلا ئائىلە تەربىيەسى، بالىنى كىچىكىدىن چاڭ تۇتۇش كېرەك. جەمئىيەتكە بەر قارىغە، ئادەم ياقمىسنى چىشلىمەي ئامال يوق . بۇ تاتلىق نەشپۈتكەن، دوختۇرخانىنىڭ ئالدىدىن ئالدىڭىزمۇ؟ يېقىندا چوڭ ئوغلۇمنىڭ مەكتىپىدە ئىككى بالا چۇمادو يەپ ئۆلۈپ قاپتۇ، سۇرۈشتۈرسەم، ئىككىمىسى ئاتا–ئانىسى ئاجرىشىپ كەتكەن بالارىكەن. كۈندە كەچتە قاۋاقلاردىن چىقالمايدىغان قىزلارنىڭمۇ يا ئانىسى يوق، يا دادىسى. رايونمىزنىڭ مەملىكەت بويىچە ئاجرىشىش نىسبىتى ئەڭ يۇقىرى رايون ئىكەنلىكىنى بىلەمسىز؟

ھېلىقى ھۇجۇمچى ئىككى ئادەمدىن ئۆتمەكچى بولۇپ، بىرىدىن ئۆتەلمىدى. دەرزە سىرتىدىكى ئاق ئاسماندا، بىر تال ئۇچار شەھەرنى ئايلىنىپ ئۇچماقتا ئىدى. مېنىڭ تاماكا چەككۈم ۋە سەگىم كەلىۋاتاتتى.

— دىققەت قىلسىڭىزلا، نورمال ئائىلىدە چوڭ بولغان زىيالىي بىلەن كەمتۈك ئائىلىدە چوڭ بولغان زىيالىينىڭمۇ ئوخشىمايدىغانلىقىنى كۆرەلەيسىز. مانا بۇ پۈتكۈل ماجرانىڭ مەنبەسى. زىيالىبىلار قانداقتۇر يېڭىلىقچى، ئەنئەنىچى ياكى ئۆچى بوڭچى دەپ ئەمەس، پەقەت ئۇنداق ئائىلىدىن كېلىپ چىققان ياكى بۇنداق ئائىلىدىن دەپ ئىككىكگە بۆلۈنىدۇ. بۇ ئىككى تەرەپ قەتئىي چىقىشالمايدۇ لېكىن خەلق زىيالىيلار بىر–بىرىنى كۆرەلمىدى دەپلا چۈشىنىدۇ.

كامران تېلىفونىننىڭ توك قاچىلىغۇچىسىنى تامدىكى چاتقۇچ تۆشۈككىگە كۆچەپ تىقتى.

— سىزمۇ ئىشلىرىڭىزنى بىر قاتار رەتكە سېلىۋېلىڭ جۇمۇ، ئاكىڭىز ھازىرغىچە سىزدىن رازى ئەمەس.

ئۇلارنىڭ گېپىنى ئۆزۈپ قويماي دەپ، گەپ قىلمايلا ئورنۇمدىن تۇرۇپ، دوختۇرخانا ھاجەتخانىسىغا چىقتىم.

سۈيدۈك قاچىسىدا بىر كۆك ماڭقا ساقغان پېتى قېتىپ قالغاندى. سۈيدۈكۈم سىبرىق كەلىۋاتاتتى. ئىسسىقىم ئېشىپ كەتكەنمىدۇ؟ تاماكا ئىسى قاڭسىق پۇراق ئارىسىغا ئاستا يېيىلدى. قولۇمنى يۇيدۈم، ئاغزىمنى چايقىدىم. كارىدوردا مېڭىۋۇتۇپ، ئىشتىنىمنىڭ سىيىرتمىسىنى ئەتتىممۇ يوق دەپ ئىچىمنى سىلاپ باقتىم. زالدىكى ئەڭ ئىنچىكە ئاۋازدىن ئەڭ ست ئاۋازغىچە ھەممىنى ئېنىق ھېس قىلماقتا ئىدىم. قوشۇق قاچىغا سۈركەلدى، ئوكۇللار چاقىلدى، دەرزە ئېچىۋېتىلدى، بىر دوختۇر ئۆزىنىڭ ئامالسىزلىقىنى ئاچچىقلىنىش بىلەن

ئاشكارىلىدى. دەل شۇ ۋاقىتتا، ماڭا يالتىلاقارىغان سپىسترا مىبنىڭ باشلانغۇچتىكى هېلىقى ساۋاقدىشىم شۇمۇ ئەمەس؟ بايىتىنقى قاڭسىق پۇراق ياتاقخانىدىن ئۇزۇلمەي كېپىلۆۋاتقان زارلىنىش ۋە قويۇق ئوكۇل هىدى بىلەن ئارىلىشىپ كەتتى. كامرانىڭ ئېيتىشىچە، يىگٌى تۇغۇلغان بوۋاق نۇرغا ماسلىشالمىغانلىقتىن كۆندۈزى كۆپ ئۇخلايدىكەن، شۇڭا يىغلاشقا كېچىلا قالىدىكەن.

مۇسابىقە ئاخىرلىشاي دېگەندى، نەتىجە يەنىلا ئىككىدە بىر ئىدى.

– بولدۇ، مەن خوتۇن–بالىلارنى ئۇرۇنلاشتۇرۇۋەتكەندىن كېيىن سىزگە تېلېفون قىلىمەن.

– ماقۇل، ئەمسە قالغان گەپنى شۇ ۋاقىتتا دېيىشەيلى، خەيرى–خوش!

بايىتىنقى دەرۋازىۋۇن بىر تالاي ئامانلىق قوغداش بۇيۇملىرى ئارىسىدا مۆگدەۋاتاتتى.

– بىردەم ماڭساق قانداق؟

ماڭدۇق. مىڭغۇۋاتاتتۇق. قىسقىلا ماڭاتتۇق. بەزىدە سۆزلىشىپ ماڭاتتۇق، بەزىدە ئۇن–تىنسىز مىڭىپ كېتەتتۇقكى، ئاياق تۈشۈشمىز بىلەن ئىشتەنممزنىڭ شىرىلدىشىدىن باشقا ئاۋاز چىقارمايتتۇق. بەزىدە تام ئۈستىدىكى بىر مۈشۈككە ئۇچرايتتۇق–دە، كامران «ھەي مۈشۈك!» دەپ چاقىراتتى. ئاندا–ساندا تونۇشلار قول ئېلىشىپ كۆرۈشۈپ ئۆتۈپ كېتەتتى. كېپىتشى ھامان كامران ماڭا بۇ ئادەمنىڭ ئارقا كۆرۈنىشىنى ئېيتىپ بېرەتتى. بەزىدە بىر توكٌلاتقۇنىڭ ئىغىزىنى ئاچقانچە، شۇ توكٌلاتقۇدەك ھاۋۇپقىسىپ تۇرۇپ قالاتتۇق. بەزىدە بىر چوڭ يوڭ ماشىنىسىنىڭ رىشاتكىلار تالىشىپ كىچىككىنە قالغان يول بۆلىكىدىن قانداقلارچە بىر قىسقۇچپاقىدەك قايرىلىغانلىقىنى تاماشا قىلاتتۇق. بەزىدە چىرايلىق قاشالانغان ئۆستەڭ بويىدىكى بىر راۋاقتا ئولتۇرۇپ ئارام ئالاتتۇق.

راۋاقنىڭ ئۇرۇندۇق، تۆۋرۈكلىرىنى قوش يۈرەك بىلەن ئىسىم، مەينەت سۆز بىلەن تېلېفون نومۇرلىرى بىر ئالغاندى. سەل نېرىراقتا، قارا كۆز ئەينەك تاقىۋالغان بىر ئادەم، بويىنىغا گالستۇك ئېسىۋالغان بىر قانچە مەكتەپ بالىلىرىمۇ ئولتۇراتتى. ئۇلارنىڭ ئىچىدىكى قارماقتا يۇقىرى يىللىقتا ئوقۇيدىغاندەك كۆرۈنىدىغان بىرسى قولىدىكى چۇۇق بىلەن ئۆزى بىلەن تەڭ دېمەتلىك يەنە بىر قىزنى ساۋۇندى: ۋايجان!

– يېقىندىن بىرى توختىماي بالىلىقىمدىكى ئىشلارنى ئەسلەيدىغان بولۇپ قالدىم. بولۇپمۇ ھەر ئاخشىمى كۆزۈمنى يۇمغىنىمدا، پۈتكۈل كۆرۈنۈشلەر كۆز ئالدىمغا كېلىۋېلىپ ئارام بەرمەيدۇ.

– مەن بالىلىقىمنى ئەسلىمەيمەن.

بایاتینقی ئوغۇل بالا قولىدىكى چىۋىق بىلەن كىچىك بالىلارغا «ماۋۇنى ئوقۇپ بىقىڭلارچۇ» دەپ خەنزۇچە خەتلەرنى كۆرسىتىۋاتاتتى.

— ۋو ئەینى، ۋو ئەینى، ۋو ئەینى...

— ماۋۇچۇ؟

— ۋو ئەینى، ۋو ئەینى...

— مانى دەیمە!

— ۋو ئەینى...

ئۇ مەیلى قایسىلا خەتنى كۆرسەتمىسۇن، بالىلار پەقەت ئاشۇ سۆزنىلا تەكرارلاپ چۆرقىرىشاتتى، كۈلۈشەتتى.

— تاماكا ئالە.

ئۇنىڭ تاماكا قېپىدا بىر تاللا تاماكا قالغاندى. مەن ئۆزۈمنىڭ ئەسكى تاماكىسىنى چىقىرىپ ئۇنىڭغا تەڭلىدىم:

— سىلەپ قوي ئۇنى، بىر تال تاماكا دېگەن ھامان لازىم بولىدۇ.

— ھەممە شۇنداق ئىنىق، شۇنچىلىك ئىنىق. ئەڭ كىچىك دېتاللىرىغىچە، ئەڭ ئەرزىمەس نەرسىلەرگىچە، ئەینى ۋاقىتتىكى دېئالوگلارمۇ ئۆز پېتى. باغلار، ئۆیلەر، ئۇیۇنلار... ھەتتا یۈگەكتىكى چىۋغىنىمۇ ئەسلىیەلەۋاتىمەن. بۇلارنىڭ شۇنچە یىللاردىن بېرى كاللامنىڭ قايسىبىر بۇرجەكىدە ساقلىنىپ قالغىنىغا ھەیرانمەن.

بىزنىڭ تاماكا چەككىنىمىزنى كۆرگەن ھېلىقى ئادەم یېنىمىزغا كېلىپ، قارا كۆز ئەینىكىنىڭ چوڭقۇرىدىن ئوت سورىدى.

— بۆشۈككە چىڭ تېڭىپ قويۇپ چىقىشىپ كەتكىنىدە، بۆشۈكنىڭ تۆتقۆچىغا ۋە تورۇسقا قاراپ یاتقاندىكى بىئارامچىلىقتا، زېرىككىنىمدىن ئانام قاچان قايتىپ كېلىپ مېنى یېشەر دەپ ئویلىغانلىرىم، قۇیاش نۇرى پەردىلەرنى یۇپپۇرۇق یورۇتقان بىر ئەتىگەنى، قۇپقۇرۇق ئۆیدە ئۆزۈم یالغۇز ئويغانغىنىم ۋە كارىۋاتتىن چۈشۈپ ھويلىغا چىققىنىم، بىر مەزگىل ئىچ-ئىچىمدىن ئۆرتىنىپ یىغلاشقا خۇمار بولۇپ قالغىنىم، تۈنجى قېتىم یولدىن ئېزىپ قالغىنىم، كەچلىرى ھۆزۈر بىلەن سوغۇق یۇتقانىغا شۇڭغۇپ كىرگىنىم ۋە ئۈیقۇغا كېتىشتىن ئىلگىرى

كالامدا چوقۇم پەيدا بولىدىغان قالايمىقان ئاۋازلار، يامغۇرنىڭ ھەر ۋاقىتىدىكى ۋە ھەر نەرسىدىكى پۆرقى، مەشتە گۆرۈلدەپ كۆيۈۋاتقان ئوتنىڭ تامدىكى شولىسى... ھەممىسى بىر كىنودەك قويۇلىدۇ.

‏– تۈنجى قېتىم سۈت كەمپۇت يېگەندە قانداق بولغاندىڭ؟

‏– كۆڭلۈم ئېلىشقان.

‏– مېنىڭمۇ شۇ!

‏– چوڭ بولۇپ بىلدىمكى، پۈتكۈل ھايۋاناتنىڭمۇ كۆڭۈل ئەڭ ئېلىشىدىغان يېرى ئەڭ مېزىلىككەن.

مەن ئۇنىڭغا بۇلارنى خاتىرىلەپ قويۇش ياكى ئۇنگە ئېلىۋېلىش تەكلىپىنى بەردىم.

‏– «قارىغۇلار شەھىرى» دەپ بىر سېنارىيە يېزىۋاتىمەن. – دېدى.

‏– ئېسسسسل!

‏– بىر شەھەر بار، پۈتۈن قارىغۇلار ياشايدۇ. ئۇلار ئاتا–بوۋىسىدىن باشلاپ قارىغۇ، ھەممىسى تۇغۇلىشىدىنلا قارىغۇ تۇغۇلىدۇ يەنە سەرتتەنمۇ قارىغۇلار كۆپلەپ تۆرىدۇ. بۇ شەھەر پۈتۈنلەي قارىغۇلار ئۈچۈن لايىھەلەنگەن، يوللىرى، بىنالىرى، زاۋۇتلىرى...بۇلارنىڭ قارىغۇلار يېزىقى بار، قارىغۇلار قانۇنى ۋە تىجارىتى بار، ئىشلەپچىقىرىشى ئاساسەن قول ھۈنەرۋەنچىلىك، كۆزى ئوچۇقلار دۇنياسىغا ئېكسپورت قىلىپمۇ تۆرىدۇ، بۇنىڭ بەدىلىگە ئۆزى قىلالمايدىغان بىر قىسىم ئىمپورت مەھسۇلاتلىرىغا ئېرىشىدۇ. ئۇ دۇنيادىن يەنە ئىنژېنېر، مۈتەخەسسىسلەر كېلىپ بۇلارنىڭ شەھەر قۇرۇلۇشىغا يارىدەم بېرىپ تۆرىدۇ. بالىلىرى كىچىكىدىن باشلاپ قارىغۇلار مائارىپىدا تەربىيەلىنىدۇ. نەرسىلەر سىيپىلىپ تونۇتۇلىدۇ، ھۈنەرلەر قولمۇ–قول ئۆگىتىلىدۇ. مەكتەپ پۈتتۈرگەندە، بالىلار ئۆزى خالىغان بىر كەسپنى تاللايدۇ. گەرچە ساناقلىقلا تاللاش بولسىمۇ لېكىن بەلگىلەنگەن كەسپلىرىنىڭ ھەرقانداق بىرى كەمسىتىلمەيدۇ، مەيلى ئىسشچى بولسۇن، مەيلى ھۆكۈمەت خادىمى ياكى ئاشپەز ياكى ناخشچى ياكى تەرجىمان ياكى يازغۇچى ياكى پاھىشە... بۇلار كىچە–كۈندۈزنى پەرق ئېتەلمىگەنلىكتىن، سائىتى ھەر ئىشنىڭ ۋاقتىنى ئەسكەرتىپ تۆرىدۇ، ھەر توچكىدا مۆئەييەن پائالىيەتنى يۈرگۈزىدۇ. قوللىرىدىكى بۇ كىچىك سائەتنى چوڭ بىر ساھەت باشقۇرىدۇ. ئاساسەن، بۇلارنىڭ ھەممە نەرسىسى يۈكسەك بىرلىككە كەلگەن، ئۇخشاش قانۇنىيەتكە بويسۇنىدۇ، ئۇخشاش يولدا ماڭىدۇ، ئۇخشاش كىيىنىدۇ ياكى كىيىنمەيدۇ، ئۇخشاش ھېسسىياتتا بولىدۇ، ئۇخشاش تىپمىلاردا سۆزلىشىدۇ. شۇنداق بولۇشىغا قارماي، بۇ شەھەردە يەنىلا قارىغۇ ئالدامچىلار، قارىغۇ ئوغرىلار ۋە پېرىخون، سېھىرگەرلەرمۇ مەۋجۇت... بىر كۈنى، بىر تون نىسبىدە، بۇ شەھەردە ھەم قارىغۇ ھەم گاس بىر

بوۋاق دۇنياغا كېلىدۇ ۋە بىر كەپچىدىلا قىزىق نۇقتىغا ئايلىنىدۇ. چوڭ-كىچىك تاراتقۇلار بۇ ئىشنى ئىز قوغلاپ خەۋەر قىلىشىدۇ، ئالىملار ئەرسىيەت نۇقتىسىدا تۇرۇپ، زادى قەيەردىن خاتالىق چىققانلىقىنى تەتقىق قىلىشىدۇ. بۇ بالىنى قانداق ئۆگىتىش مۇمكىن؟ پۈتۈن شەھەر ئەندىشىگە چۆمىدۇ...

– ئىسسسسل، ئاندىنچۇ؟

– تېخى مۇشۇنچىلىك يازدىم.

– پەيزى كىنو بولغىدەك جۇمۇ، دىنىچۇ؟ دىنى بارمۇ؟

– كۆپىنچە ئادەملىرى دىنسىز، بىر قىسىم كىشىلىرى قاراڭغۇلۇق تەگرىسىگە ئىشىنىدۇ. ئۇلار تەكرى قاراڭغۇلۇقتا بولغاچقا، بىزنى قارىغۇ قىلىش ئارقىلىق ئۆزىگە يېقىنلاتقان دەپ بىلىدۇ. يەنە بىر قىسىم كىشىلەر يورۇقلۇق تەگرىسىگە ئېتىقاد قىلىدۇ، ئۇلار تەكرىننىڭ ئەھكامىغا بويسۇنسا، ئۆلگەندىن كېيىن كۆزىنىڭ ئېچىلىدىغانلىقىغا، بارچە رەڭلەرنى ۋە نۇرنى كۆرەلەيدىغانلىقىغا ئىشىنىدۇ. ئەلۋەتتە، بۇ پەقەت ئاۋۇ بوۋاق تۇغۇلۇشتىن بۇرۇنقى ئىشلار...

– ئۇ بوۋاقنى پەيغەمبەر قىلىپ يېزىشنى ئويلاۋاتمايدىغانسەن-ھە؟

– ياق، پەيغەمبەر ئەمەس... بىراق مۇشۇنداقراق بىر نەرسە، ئىشقىلىپ ئۇخشىمايدۇ.

– ئۇ يەنە ئاشىق بولۇشى كېرەك، مۇھەببەت ھېكايىسى بولمىسا كەم كۆرىدۇ دەيسەن.

– كىنو بىشىغا مۇنداق مۇقەددىمە سۆزى بېرىلىدۇ: ساتۇانىڭ بۇددىغا* كىرىشى بىرسىننىڭ قاراڭغۇلۇققا كىرىشىگە ئوخشايدۇكى، ئۇندا بىر نىمەنى ئالغا قىلغىلى بولماس. –ۋاجرا نومى، 14-پارە.

– قارغۇلار ئۈچۈن ئىشلەنگەن كىنونى قارغۇلار كۆرەلمەيدۇ، قىزىق ئىش-دە.

– قارغۇلار چۈشىدە نېمە كۆرەر؟

بىز تۇرۇۋاتقان ياغاچ كۆۋرۈكنىڭ ئاستىدىن سۇ ئېقىۋاتاتتى. يىراقتىن بىر قارا بۇلۇت بىسىپ كېلىۋاتاتتى. خارەتخاندىن ئاڭلىنىۋاتقان تىلىش ماشىنىسىنىڭ ئاۋازى شۇنچىلىك خۇش ياقتى. ئالدىمىزدىكى يولغا چىقىپ تاكسى توسماقچى بولدۇق. ئىستولبىننىڭ ئۈستىدە بىر قاغا قانات قاقتى.

– قاق قاق قاق، ئاۋۇ قاغا بىزنى تونۇدى ئاداش.

پلاستىنكا ساتقۇچىلار چۆلدەرىگەن دۇكانلىرىدا ئولتۇرۇشاتتى، ئەينى ۋاقىتتىكى قاينام–تاشقىنلىقتىن ئەسەرمۇ يوق ئىدى. شۇ چاغلاردىكى مېدىيا ئىشلىرىنىڭ گۈللىنىشىنى ئۇلاردىن ئايرىپ قارىغىلى بولمايتتى. ئون يىللار ئاۋۋال، ئالدىغا لىق ئادەم توپلىشىۋېلىپ، بەش–ئالتە تېلېۋىزوردىن قويۇلۇۋاتقان ئوخشىمىغان كىنولارنى كۆرۈۋاتقان بۇنداق دۇكانلارنى ھەر قانداق بىر كوچىدا ئۇچراتقىلى بولاتتى. ئەممىدە قىلىشىچە، بىر پلاستىنكىنىڭ كۆنلۈك ئارىيەت ئېلىش ھەققى ئىككى سوم ئىدى. «بىگتۇۋەن» دېدى كامران، قولى بىلەن كۆرسەتمەيلا. ئىچىدە بۇلجۇڭ گۆشلىرى پۇلتىيىپ چىققان ٠٠ر چۇپ جۇڭخۇا ئوغۇا ،–قىزىنىڭ مىس ھەيكىلى قەد كۆتۈرۈپ تۇراتتى. شەھەرنىڭ ئاسفالت يوللىرى تار تېرەكلىك كوچىلار بىلەن ئاخىرلىشاتتى.

– تېلېفون تىترەۋاتامدۇ؟

– ياق.

يولنىڭ قارشى تەرىپىدىكى دەرۋازىدىن كالىچىنى پالاقلاتقىنىنچە بىر بالا چىقىپ كەلدى. بۇ تەرەپتە بىرى ئۆنتۈغا ئىسقىرتىپ، ئۇلارنىڭ نەقەدەر يېقىن مۇناسىۋەتتە ئىكەنلىكىنى ئىپادىلىدى. ئۇ بالا بولسا، شۇك، يېقىن ئەتراپتا دادام بار دېگەندەك ئىشارەت قىلدى. ئۇنىڭ كەينىدە كۆزلىرى قىپقىزىل بىر خوراز ئۆنتۈغا تىكىلىپ تۇراتتى. كامران ماڭا بىر نەرسە دەۋاتاتتى .

– نېمە دېدىڭ؟

– قۇشلارنىڭ كۆزىدىكى بىزنى دەيمەن، ئۇلارغا زادى قانداق ۋەكرۇنىدىغاندىممىز؟

– بىلمەيمەن، خۇددى ئۇلڭ كۆزى بىلەن سول كۆزى ئوخشاش بىر نەرسىنى كۆرمەيۋاتقاندەك، ئۇلار بىشىنى ئىككى ياقىا چۆرۈپ قايتا–قايتا قارايدۇ. مەن توردىن ئاختۇرۇپ باقاي–ھە.

– كۆرۈنۈش، – دېدى كامران، – نەرسەلەردىن قايىتقان ئەكس نۇرنىڭ كۆز پەردىمىزگە يىغىلىپ، شەكىللەندۈرگەن تەتۈر سۈرەت ئۇچۇرىنىڭ نۇر سەزگۈچ ھۇجەيرىلەر ئارقىلىق مېڭىدىكى كۆرۈۋ مەركىزىگە يىتىپ بىرىشى ۋە كۆرۈۋ تىلىدا ئوقۇلۇشى. كۆزىمىزنىڭ ئىپقى ھەم قارىسى بار، ئىپقى قارىسىنى قوغدايدۇ، قارىسىنىڭ ئەتراپى نۇرنى سومۇرىدۇ، مەركىزى زۇلمەتنى ساقلايدۇ. يەنە مىڭە ئۇستى بىزى دەپ بىر يەر بار، بۇ ئىنساننىڭ ئۇچىنچى كۆزى دەپ ئاتىلمىدۇ. ئىنسان خىيالىي كۆرۈنۈشلەرنى دەل مۇشۇ يەردىن كۆرىدۇ، ئۇلۇش ئالدىدا كۆرۈندىغانلىرىمۇ مۇشۇ يەرنىڭ پەۋقۇلئاددە جانلىنىپ كېتىشى بىلەن مۇناسىۋەتلىك ئىكەن. ئىشقىلىپ، كۆرۈشتە ئۇبىيىكتىپلىق بىلەن سۇبىيىكتىپلىق تەڭلا مەۋجۇت. مۇنداقچە ئېيتقاندا، ئىنسان كۆرگەنلىكى نەرسە كۆرۈستلىگەن نەرسە.

— نېمىننىڭ كۆرسەتكىنى؟ مىگىننىگمۆ؟

— كۆرۈش تىلىدا نېمە ئوقۇتقان بولسا شۇنىڭ كۆرسەتكىنى بولماي؟!

— ۋىكىپىدادا دېيىلىشىچە، قۇشلار بىنەپشە نۇرنى كۆرەلەيدىكەن، كۆرۈش نۇقتىسى كۆپۈنكى ئەينەكنىڭكىگە ئوخشاپ كېتەرمىش. — دېدىم مەن، — ئاۋۇ تەرەپتىن ماڭامدۇق، قىزىل چىراغ يېنىپ قاپتۇ.

— بىزگە ھەممە تەرەپ يېشىل.

بىزگە ھەممە تەرەپ قاراڭغۇ. يول قىرىدىكى سىمونت قاشتا ئۇلتۇرۇپ، خۇددى يېڭى بىر ھاياتقا ئاپىرىدىغاندەك تەقەززالىق بىلەن تاكسىننىڭ كېلىشنى كۈتتۈق. قاشنىڭ ئارقا تەرىپىدىكى ئېرىق ئەخلەتلەر بىلەن تولدۇرۇۋېتىلگەنىدى.

— ئەخلەتلەر: رەخت پارچىسى، شىشە پارچىسى، كېسەك پارچىسى، تاماكا كۆيۈكى، نان كۆيۈكى، كىتاب كۆيۈكى، بانان شۆپۈكى، گازىر شۆپۈكى، تۆخۈم شاكىلى، قۇم قەغىزى، ھەيز قەغىزى، شاكىلات قەغىزى، ئاق يالتىراق، قارا يالتىراق، قىزىل يالتىراق، ئالما قىپپى...

— ئالما قىپپى؟

— ئالما تېلىفونننىڭ ئەمەس، ئالما مېۋىسىنىڭ. ياستۇق قىپپى، قۇلۇلە قىپپى، تۇخۇ سۆڭىكى، ئېڭەك سۆڭىكى، تىل سۆڭىكى...

— تىل سۆڭىكى؟

— ھا،ھا،ھا... چاقچاق، تۆشۈك مونچاق، تۆشۈك پايپاق، تۆشۈك گاندون، ئېتىلغان توپ، ئېتىلغان قوناق، ئېتىلغان يۇڭ، ھەرە تېغى، ساقال تېغى، كەتمەن تېغى، سۈ قۈتىسى، سۈ كارتىسى، سۈ تاپانچىسى...

شۇپۈرنىڭ پېشانىسىگە ئاپتاپ ۋە ئۇنىڭ مايلىق چېچى تەڭلا چاپلىشىپ تۇراتتى. تاكسى ئىشىكىنى قاتتىق يېپىپ سالدىم.

ماشىنىدا ئاۋۇال بىر ئىسلامىي ناخشا قويۇلدى، ئاندىن «ئۇيغۇر دېگەن مۇشۇنداق» دېگەن ناخشا قويۇلدى. كامران ئىسلامىي ناخشلار بىلەن ئۇسۇللۇق ناخشلارنىڭ قانداق ئىنچىكە مۇناسىۋەتنى بارلىقى توغرىسىدا سۆزلىدى. مەن بۇ خىل ناخشلارغا ئۆزۈمنىڭ نەقەدەر ئۆچلۈكىمنى ھېس قىلدىم. دۆت مۇزىكا! دۆتلۈكمىدىن خۇددى توپا ئارىلاشتۇرۇلغان قايماقتا ياكى چاندۇرماي قويۇۋېتىلگەن ئۇسۇرۇۋققىلا ئوخشايدۇ.

– ئاشقۇنلۇقمۇ بىر ئۇسسۇللۇق ناخشا! – دەپ ۋارقىرىدى كامران.

– رادىئو ئاڭلايلىچۇ؟

شوپۇر رادىئونى ئاچتى.

– ياخشىمۇ سىز؟

– ئەسسالامۇ–ئەلەيكۇم، مەن بىر ناخشا تەلەپ قىلاي دېگەن.

– ۋەئەلەيكۇم ئەسسالام، قايسى ناخشىنى تەلەپ قىلاي دەيسىز؟

– «ئايدىڭ ئاخشام» دېگەن ناخشىنى، ئابدۇسوپۇرنىڭ.

– «ئايدىڭ ئاخشام»... كەچۈرۈڭ، بۇ ناخشا بۈگۈن ئۇرۇنلاشتۇرۇلغان ناخشىلار تىزىملىكىدە يوق.

– ھە...مەن...چەتتىم... شۇڭا...

سىگنالنىڭ چاتىقىمىكىن، ئاۋاز ياخشى ئاڭلانماي قالدى. شوپۇر قانالنى يۆتكىدى.

– ...(ئايال دكتور ئاۋازى) ھارپىسىنى قىزغىن كۆتۈۋېلىش يۈزىسىدىن، نۇرلۇق يېزىسىدىكى ئۈچ مىڭغا يېقىن دېھقان يېزا باشقارمىسىنىڭ ئارقىسىدىكى كەڭرى مەيدانغا يىغىلىپ كەچىك ئالما ئۇسسۇلى ئوينىدى. بۇ مەملىكەتىمىزدە ئەڭ كۆپ ئادەم قاتناشقان كەچىك ئالما ئۇسسۇلى بولۇش بىلەن بۇ تۈردە يېڭى رېكورت ياراتتى. زىيارىتىمىزنى قوبۇل قىلغان سەكسەن ياشلىق بوۋاي توختى مەتقادىر مۇنداق دېدى: (ئەر دكتور ئاۋازى) بەكلا ھاياجانلاندىم، بۇ پائالىيەت بەكلا ياخشى ئۆتكۈزۈلدى، بايرامنى كۆتۈۋېلىپلا قالماي، كۈندىلىك تۇرمۇشىمىزنى بېيىتتى. ئىناقلىق، ھەمدەملىكىمىزنى ئاشۇردى. بۇ خىل پائالىيەتلەرنىڭ كۆپلەپ ئۆتكۈزۈلۈپ تۇرۇشىنى چىن كۆڭلۈمدىن ئۈمىد قىلىمەن. (ئايال دكتور ئاۋازى) ئىختىيارى مۇخبىرىمىز ياسىنجان تەلمۇئالدى خەۋىرى...

ماشىنا نۇرغۇن ئادەم تاكسى تالىشىپ قوللىرىنى سوزۇۋاتقان جايدا توختىدى. كامران ماڭا دۇكاننىڭ ئورنىنى ئېيتىپ بەردى، ئۇ ئەمدى قايتىمسا بولمايتتى. يەر ئاستى ئۆتۈشمە يولىدىن ئىككى خەنزۇ قىزى مېڭىپ چىقتى. مەن ئۇلارنىڭ ئارىسىدىكى قىزىل ئېگىز پاشنىلىق ئاياغ بىلەن قارا خۇرۇم ئىشتان كىيىۋالغان بىرسىگە دىققەت قىلدىم. كامران بىر گەپنى «خەنزۇچە نېمە دەيتتى؟» دەپ مەندىن سورىدى. ئۇدۇل تەرەپتىكى ساقچى ماشىنىسىنىڭ چىرىغى ئۇپچۇرىسىدىكى ھاۋانى ئالا–يېشىل ياندۇرماقتا ئىدى. ئەتىگەننىڭ ياقى قانچە تال تاماكا چېكىپ

بولدۇق؟ يەنە قاچان كۆرۈشىمىز؟ ئىشلار راستتىنلا دېگىنىمىزدەك بولامدۇ؟ يۈزلەرنى چالا توك بېسىپ كەتكەن بىر قارامتۇل كىشى بىزگە قولىدىكى تېلېفوننىڭ سوغۇق ئېكرانىنى گويا بىر جاۋابنى كۆرسەتكەندەك كۆرسىتىپ دېدى:

– ئالامسىز؟

سودا سارىيىننىڭ ئېغىزى يېنىغا تىكلەپ قويۇلغان كىچىك ئېلان تاختىسىدىكى ئايالنىڭ ئوچۇق بەدىنى بىر كەملەر تەرىپىدىن جىجىۋېتىلگەن ئىدى. قولۇمدا تەكشۈرۈش ماشىنىسىدىن ئۆتكۈزگۈدەك بىر سومكىنىڭ يوقلۇقىدىن خىجالەت بولدۇم ۋە يۈگۈرگەن پېتى پەشتاقتىن چۈشۈپ، دۈكىننى تاقاي دەپ تۇرغان كۆز ئەينەكلىك دۇكاندارغا ئېيىتتىم:

– ماڭا بىر كامېرا كېرەك، مەن ھەممىنى ئەڭ سەممىي رەۋىشتە خاتىرىلىمەكچى.

*ساتۇۋا: مەخلۇقات، بەندە.

بۆددى: ئۇيغانماق، ئارىفقا يەتمەك.

2016–يىلى 1–،2–،3–،4–،5–،6–،7–ئايلار.

Translator's Note: Inspired by the saturation of surveillance cameras in East Turkistan, this story explores the implications of all that is seen and watched. Through the translation process of this piece, we became aware of how we are constantly being gazed at, from the interplay of light and colour to the mechanisms of visual perception, from the literal bird's-eye to the scrutinising lenses of police and divine authority. Even names reflect the theme of seeing. The unnamed protagonist seeks to reconcile the camera's unblinking gaze with his own sense of identity and agency. As we read, we reflect on the pervasive control exerted by the Chinese Communist Party's surveillance apparatus, on how we perceive ourselves, and on the ways in which being watched shapes our lives.

Camera

Merdan Eheteli

Translation | Munawwar Abdulla

It was time to record it all, as honestly as possible. I changed into my white boxers, which I had washed in case I'd meet Tangnur. I applied the perfume I'd received on my birthday three years ago, combed my hair the same way I had done that day, and set off to buy a camera. Summer had just about started. All that was bright this morning was the air, the front door of our neighbour – a dog owner – and the colour on the skirt of someone walking by with food. All that was dark were the expression of the fruit seller on the street, the shackles of the steelyard, and his unknown thoughts.

"Allah is watching me", "Raziye is a slut", "Don't dump trash here if you're human…" read the scribbles on the wall under which three boys were playing. I don't know why, but all little boys look drunk to me, and every time I get drunk, I ask myself: Wasn't I just like this when I was little? Forehead feverish, ears deaf, mouth half open, my focus concentrated on one point, numb to my surroundings. In all my photos as a kid, my cheeks are as red as the flag in the sun, my eyes teasing like the flag of the night, looking at the camera as though I am dreaming.

My body shivered slightly in the wind. Walking towards me like ants were a group of students in uniform. The scents of bread and kawap exhumed from tannours followed me for quite a while. Passing one by one before my eyes, were youth squatting on all corners of the streets, their hands outstretched, smirking and waiting to be examined; women sitting on tall chairs throwing doogh high in the air; cobblers poking awls furiously into wrinkled sandals, sitting with their backs to the park, and young wives sitting barefoot in front of them with their other sandal in hand; groups of hired hands gambling while they waited for their employer; yoghurt sellers extending their bowls at every passer-by; city council personnel twirling their hats on their fingers, sitting on confiscated electric scooters and ignoring the pleas of vehicle lessors; employees sitting on the egalitarian bus stop chairs, anxious about being late for work; and cats licking themselves in front of a stone lion that held treasure in its mouth. The green uniforms under the green trees cast suspicious looks at the red cars sitting under the red lights.

I entered a barbershop and scared myself, thinking the person's leg in front of me was mine. I entered an eatery and the ruba'i on the wall counselled me on being thankful. I entered a bank and the service machine mimicked back my Chinese pronunciation. I passed by store glass doors like a ghost, the farmer's market like a debtor, the bookshop like a memory.

All sorts of cars drove by on the road, their eyes narrowed, bulging, grinning, shocked, angry, menacing, miserable, unaware, crying. They looked different, but their appetite for a person was the same. Traffic noises crushed into my ears like waves in a shell, ringing out for some time.

As the hour hand descended, and the water level in my bottle dropped, and my mood sunk further down still, I found myself being questioned by Kamran in front of the Nur Hayat hospital.

"So, pimper, what brings you to these parts?" he said, grinning at me with his bag of pears.

"Like there is in every single corner of this city," I said to him, "I need a camera at home too. Funny thing is, there's barely any shop that sells them."

"That's because you haven't found the right spot," he said, taking out two smokes from a cigarette pack and offering one to me, "I know a place."

He knew a lot of things, an expert in market and trade. Plus, his dream was to one day drop it all and set his whole mind to filmmaking.

Cigarettes were lit; we took a deep drag and blew smoke. Our conversation consisted of the season's involuntary dirt rains, the sluggishness of business, and what we ate for lunch. I threw my cigarette butt into the flower bed on the footpath. Kamran spat on the ground with a splat, and said he had a more urgent matter to deal with, that is, he needed to take this kilo of Korla pears and visit the professor at the hospital in room 723. Then he could help me get a camera. I complied.

The gatekeeper sized us up as if he were questioning what business we had here. The building we wanted to visit was one farthest inside.

"Hospital elevators are weird, aren't they?"

"Long, narrow, dirty, pungent, rusty, dismal, ponderous, retarded, dilapidated, stubborn. As if they were made to move corpses."

We found the hospital room in no time. The professor was sitting, one hand on the phone and the other holding the hand of a woman lying in bed. He stood when he saw us and greeted us enthusiastically. His third child had been born. The television on the wall was playing a match. The score was 2-1. Kamran quit playing with the newborn and told him the baby was very cute.

"We weren't too precious about choosing the baby's name, so it's nothing to be mad about if it's forgotten," said the third-time father. It was clear that they'd spent a lot of time thinking of a name. "But it's difficult to find a unique name, and if it's too distinctive, then registering it becomes more of a hassle."

The opposing team's striker faked a fall in the penalty area. The referee didn't take notice. The screen showed a close-up focus on the striker's knotted jaw muscles. In the 90s, Manchester had a famous striker. It was rumoured that if he wasn't successful on first touch during kick-off, his expression would darken the whole match. Luck, awareness, skill, and so on never did smile upon him.

"That's right, the God that blesses you with a child also allocates their fortune. Would our Creator, who made us, place His own creation in hardship?"

"The teams' confrontation in centre field intensifies," the commentator reported.

Many years ago, a taxi driver who overheard that I was heading to my football school had turned to me and said, "I'll tell ya' this though your mother's sitting next to you, little bro. You know football, it's a game you play saying you'll fuck your opponent's mother," and stuck up his middle finger with force. I'm not sure why, but every time I think about that incident, the song "Ave Maria" rings in my ears.

"I mean, how can we not enrol the child in school? Even so, the priority is family education. A child should be managed closely from a young age. Look at society, it's hard not to bite one's collar— these pears are so sweet, did you buy them from in front of the hospital?— Recently, two boys at my eldest son's school overdosed on narcotics. When I looked into it, I found out that both their parents were divorced. The girls who spend all their nights in bars also have no mother, no father. Did you know that our region has one of the highest divorce rates in the country?"

The striker from earlier attempted to get passed two defenders but only passed one. In the white sky outside the window, a helicopter was patrolling the city. I was feeling the need to smoke and take a piss.

"If you pay close enough attention, you can see the difference between an academic who was raised in a normal family compared to one from a broken family. That there is the source of all academic disputes. Academics aren't divided by whether they are liberal or conservative or this or that, they are divided into two groups – either they're from this sort of family or that sort of family. These two sides will never get along, but society will believe that academics are just spiteful of one another."

Kamran plugged his phone's charger into a socket on the wall. "You should set your affairs in order soon as well, your brother is still not happy with you," he said.

Not wanting to interrupt their conversation, I silently stood up and went to the hospital's bathrooms.

A piece of green snot had stuck and dried in the urinal. My urine was yellow… had my dry-heat become unbalanced? Cigarette smoke spread slowly into the acrid stench. I washed my hands and rinsed my mouth. Walking down the corridor, I wondered if I'd zipped up my fly and felt my crotch. I was keenly aware of every noise in the hall, from the most shrill to the most ugly. Spoons scraped on plates, syringes quickly snapped, windows were opened, and one doctor bitterly confessed his hopelessness. Was that nurse who'd glanced back at me that classmate from primary school, back in the day? The acrid stench from earlier mixed with the steady stream of complaints and thick injection smells coming from the wards. According to Kamran, newborns haven't adjusted to the light yet and so sleep all day and leave all their crying to the night.

The match was almost over, and the score was still 2-1.

"Alright, I'll call you when I've taken care of my wife and kids."

"Sure, we'll talk more then, goodbye!"

The gatekeeper from earlier was dozing off among a bunch of peace-keeping items.

"How about we take a walk?"

We walked. We were walking. We were going to walk just a bit. Sometimes we walked in conversation, sometimes we walked in such silence, we'd make no noise but for our footsteps and the swish of our pants. Sometimes we'd come across a cat on a wall, and Kamran would call, "Hey, cat!" Here and there an acquaintance would walk by with a handshake, and as they left, Kamran would tell me their whole background. Sometimes we'd open a fridge and stand, fridge-like, agape and staring. Sometimes we entertained ourselves watching cargo trucks wresting for rail and, somehow, twisting like a crab through what small piece of road they had. And sometimes we rested in beautifully fenced pavilions near stream banks.

The chairs and columns in the pavilion had been taken up by inscribed double hearts with names, dirty words, and phone numbers. A bit further away sat a man with dark glasses, and a group of school kids with neckerchiefs. One of the kids who seemed like they could be from an older year level used the twig in his hand to whip a girl who looked the same age: Ouch!

"These days I cannot stop thinking about things from my childhood. Especially at night, when I close my eyes, all these scenarios appear before me and won't give me peace."

"I don't think about my childhood."

The boy was using his twig to point at Chinese characters, asking the younger kids to try reading them.

"Wo aini, wo aini, wo aini…"

"How about this?"

"Wo aini, wo aini…"

"I said this!"

"Wo aini…"

No matter what he pointed at, the kids would only repeat that phrase, yelling and laughing.

"Take a smoke."

There was only one left in the cigarette box.

I took my own subpar cigarette and held it to him. "Put that away, you'll need a good cigarette soon."

"Everything is clear, so clear. To the tiniest details, the most insignificant thing, the exact same dialogue as before. The orchards, houses, games – I can even remember the time I was swaddled. I am shocked that these memories have been stored in whatever crevice of my brain for so many years."

The man from earlier saw us smoking and walked over, asking for a light from deep behind his black sunglasses.

"My feelings of agitation when I was left wrapped tightly into my cradle, staring at the ceiling and the cradle handle; the boredom I felt wondering when my mother would come and unwrap me; the morning where the sun lit the curtains so brightly; the time I woke up to a completely empty house and got out of bed to go to our yard; the phase where I'd become addicted to weeping from the depths of my heart; the first time I got lost; the nights where I'd dive into my cold blankets with joy, and the chaotic voices that were bound to enter my head before I'd fall asleep; the unique smells of rain at every time and on every thing; the shadows of the flames crackling in our stove… they play out like a movie in my head."

"How was it the first time you tried a milk candy?"

"I felt sick."

"Likewise!"

"I realised when I got older, the most delicious part of all the animals in the world is the most nauseating part."

I proposed that he should write all this down or keep a voice recording of everything.

"I'm writing a script called *City of the Blind*," he said.

"Niiiice!"

"There's this city, and everyone who lives there is blind. They've been blind for generations. They're born blind, and blind people from outside also come to live there. This city was designed specifically for blind people, its roads, buildings, factories… They have a writing system for blind people, laws and businesses for the blind. For the most part, they trade in handcrafts. They even export out to the seeing world, and in return they import products that they can't make themselves. Engineers and specialists from that world also come and help build and upkeep this city. The children are brought up with blind education from a young age. Objects are recognised through touch, skills are taught from hand to hand. When they finish school, the children pick their career paths. Although there are only a limited number to choose from, none of their choices will be looked down on, whether they are a labourer, government personnel, a chef, musician, translator, writer, or sex worker… Since they can't differentiate between night and day, their clocks prompt the time for each task, and they execute each activity at each particular point in time. The small timepieces on their wrists are controlled by a larger clock. Essentially, everything has come to a unified zenith; they obey the same laws, walk the same paths, clothe or not in the same fashion, feel the same emotions, and talk about the same subjects. Despite this, blind swindlers, thieves, witches, and magicians exist.

One day, at midnight, a baby is born who is both blind and deaf, and becomes an overnight sensation. Large and small broadcasters track the issue and inform the public, scholars conduct research from a genetic perspective, wondering what could have gone wrong. How would the child learn? The whole city is enveloped in a quandary…"

"Niiiiice, and then what?"

"That's all I've got."

"It sounds like it's going to be an amazing movie, alright. How about religion? Do they have a religion?"

"Most of them do not, but some of them believe in the god of the dark. They believe that since god is in the dark, it made them blind in order to bring them closer to itself. Another group puts their faith in a god of light. They obey its commandments and believe that when they die their eyes will open and they will be able to see light and all the colours of the spectrum. Of course, this is all before that baby is born…"

"You're not thinking of making this baby a prophet, are you?"

"No, he is not a prophet… but something similar. In any case, it's not the same."

"And he needs to fall in love, no one is gonna watch something if it's not a love story."

"At the beginning of the film I'll write this prelude: For the welfare of all living beings they should do it without relying on appearances, and without attachment. —Diamond Sutra, Chapter 14."

"It's ironic that blind people can't see a movie made for blind people."

"I wonder what blind people dream of?"

Water was running under the wooden bridge we were standing on. A black cloud was hurtling towards us from afar. The satisfying sound of a woodcutting machine was coming from the carpenter shop. We walked to the roadside and decided to hail a taxi. A crow that was perched on the telephone pole flapped its wings.

"Caw caw caw, that crow recognised us buddy."

Vinyl sellers sat in their deserted shops, not a sign left of the hustle and bustle of earlier times. Back then it was impossible to separate the flourishing entertainment industry from them. A couple of decades ago, you could find so many of these shops on every corner, playing different films on five or six televisions at the same time, with people filling up the storefront. From what I remember, it cost 2 som to rent a vinyl for a day.

"Bingtuan," said Kamran, imperceptibly. Inside, a copper statue of a Huaxia boy and girl with bulging muscles stood raised, looking invincible. The asphalt roads of the city ended with the narrow streets lined with poplars.

"Is your phone vibrating?"

"No."

A boy came over from a gate on the other side of the road, his galoshes flopping about. On this side, someone whistled, indicating how well the two were acquainted. The boy seemed to make a gesture to say, quiet, my dad is nearby. Behind him, a rooster with red eyes stood staring at him. Kamran was saying something to me.

"What did you say?"

"Us, in the eyes of birds I said. What do we look like to them?"

"I don't know, they throw their heads from side to side, over and over, as if their left and right eyes don't see the same thing. Let me look it up."

"Vision," said Kamran, "is the language of sight, which is an interpretation of light reflecting off of objects, onto the membrane of our eyes as an upside-down image, that is then processed by our occipital lobe via the photoreceptors in our retina. Our eyes have a white part and a black part. The white protects the black, the black's surroundings absorb the light, and its centre preserves the dark. There is also something called the pineal gland, and this is known as the third eye. People see their thoughts and imagination in this very spot, and the visions people get before they die is associated with its unusual activation. In any case, seeing is both objective and subjective at the same time. In other words, what people see is what they are shown."

"Shown by what? The mind?"

"It's whatever we've been taught in the language of sight, that's what shows us, isn't it?"

"According to Wikipedia, birds can see ultraviolet light, and their vision is apparently the same as a convex mirror," I said. "Should we walk on that side? The red light is on."

"For us, it's green in every direction."

For us, it was dark in every direction. We sat on the cement curb and waited eagerly for a taxi, as if it was going to take us to a new life. The stream behind the curb had been filled with trash.

"The trash: pieces of fabric, pieces of glass, pieces of brick, burnt cigarettes, burnt bread, burnt books, banana peels, sunflower seed shells, egg shells, sandpaper, sanitary pads, chocolate wrappers, white plastic bags, black plastic bags, red plastic bags, apple bags…"

"Apple Cases?"

"Not the Apple iPhones, the fruits. Pillowcases, snail shells, chicken bones, jaw bones, tongue bones…"

"Tongue bones?"

"Hahaha… just kidding, pearls with holes, socks with holes, condoms with holes, popped balls, popped corn, burst wool, saw blades, beard blades, mattock blades, water containers, water cards, water guns…"

Both the sun and the driver's oily hair were glued to his forehead. I slammed the taxi's door closed.

First an Islamic song played in the car, then *Uyghur Dégen Mushundaq*. Kamran discussed the delicate relationship between Islamic music and modern folk. I realised how much

I hated this sort of music. Stupid music! It's so idiotic it's like cream mixed with dirt, or a silent fart.

"Extremism is also a collective dance!" yelled Kamran.

"Can we listen to the radio?"

The driver turned on the radio.

"Hello?"

"Assalamu alaikum, I was hoping to request a song."

"Wa'alaykum assalam, which song would you like to request?"

"The song *Ayding Axsham* by Abdusupur."

"*Ayding Axsham…* sorry, this song is not part of our playlist today."

"Oh— I'm— that's why—"

Perhaps there was something wrong with the signal, but the sound wasn't coming through clearly. The driver switched channels.

"[a female announcer's voice] …eve being enthusiastically welcomed by almost 3,000 farmers in Nurluq, dancing the Little Apple Dance in the large square behind the village administration office. They have created a record in our country for the most number of people performing the Little Apple Dance at the same time. Toxtimet Qadir, an 80-year-old grandfather who agreed to be interviewed, commented: [a male announcer's voice] I was very excited. The event went really well. Not only did it welcome in this celebration, it enriched the quality of our daily lives. It increased peace and harmony. I sincerely hope more of these sorts of events will be organised. [Female announcer's voice] News from our freelance reporter Yasinjan Tilivaldi…"

The Little Apple Dance was a viral dance sensation in China. In East Turkistan, the government organised public dance sessions for peasants and imams to "promote social harmony" and "combat religious extremism".

The car stopped at a place where a lot of people were waving their hands, competing for a taxi. Kamran let me know the location of the store as he had to leave soon. Two Chinese girls walked out from an underground passageway. I noticed the one wearing red high heels and black leather pants. Kamran asked me how to say something in Chinese. The lights on the police car ahead of us were lighting its surroundings in garish colours. How many cigarettes had we smoked today? Would everything go the way we planned? A greyish man covered in patchy stubble held up a phone's cold screen, as if he was showing us the answer, and asked:

"Want to buy it?"

The naked body of the woman on the small billboard erected next to the mall's entrance had been graffitied by someone. Embarrassed that I didn't have a bag to put through the security scanners, I ran down the stairs to the bespectacled shopkeeper who was just about to close shop.

"I need a camera, I want to record it all as honestly as possible."

Xoten, Jan-July 2016

     UNDER THE MULBERRY TREE

From Happiness to History

Sarvenaz Nurali

Selimpaşa, Istanbul, Türkiye 2021

پاسپورت

ئابدۇشۇكۇر مۆھەممەت

(ئەسىر ئۆمۈر پاسپورتقا ئېرىشەلمىگەن
قەرىندا(شلىرىمغا بېغىشلايمەن)

گۈزەل بىر چۈش سولانغان ئىچىمگە،
قەبرىگە ئايلىنار ئۇ يەنە تۆغۆلغان يېرىدە.
ئۇرۇش يوق، ئەمما ئۆلۈم قايىنىغان شەھەردە
ماي قوڭغۇزىدەك يالتىرايدۇ ۋەھىمە.

تېنىمدىن سوزۇلۇپ چىققان سولغۇنلۇق
ئاسمان يوق، ۋاقىت يوق بىر نۇقتىدا
تەلمۈرگەنچە تامغا سىزىلغان گۈزەل كېپىلەچەككە
يوقاپ كېتەر بارا-بارا.

چىگرا بىر پارچە قەغەز
ياكى ئاققان قاننىڭ ئاخىرقى مەنزىلى.
چۆمۈلە ئۆتەلەيدىغان، لېكىن ئادەم ئۆتەلمەيدىغان
سىزىقتا
ئۆلۈم چىچەكلەيدۇ قىپقىزىل رەڭدە.

ھايات بىر ۋاراق قەغەز ۋە ئىككى قۇر خەتكە قامالغان
ئۇننىڭ ئالتۇن ئاچقۇسى ئۆلۈم ياكى نامەلۇم بىرى.

ئىھ سەرگەردان شامال
سېنىڭ ئانا ۋەتىنىڭ قەيەردە،
پاسپورتسىز كېپىلەمسەن بۇ يەرگە؟

2020-يىلى 31-ماي

Passport

Abdushukur Muhammet

*(Dedicated to my friends who
could never attain a passport)*

A beautiful dream is trapped in my body,
which becomes a graveyard in its birthplace.
In this battle devoid, death seethed city,
fear gleams like a dung beetle.

The lifelessness that stretches out from my body,
sits at a point with no sky and no time.
The more I desire the future painted on the wall,
the more it disappears.

Borders are a piece of paper,
or the final destination of coursing blood.
At the line an ant can cross, but a person can't,
death blooms the colour red.

Life is imprisoned in two sentences and one paper.
Its golden key is death or a foreigner.

Oh wind, you wanderer,
where is your motherland,
can you get there with no passport?

31 May 2020

Translation | Munawwar Abdulla

Pastoral

Jangul Baurjan

If I lived in a country that recognised me
I like to imagine life as a herder on my mountains,
surrounded by the stories of my ancestors;
to wake to the azan
and fall asleep on the lap of my apa and ata.
But I am my own country,
my body is a sacred geography.
And I recognise myself before any country.
I recognise my land before any border.
I recognise my people before any government.
I am still, despite what they say about me,
a nomad.
— me

Conversation with Contributor

JB   *I was inspired by my grandparents, their stories, their faith in a future
beyond what is given or taken for granted. I write because I want to
explore my own memories, what they mean, and how that changes
when I put it down on paper. I just wanted to sit with my longing and
grief better. If there is a message, I hope somewhere, someone feels
accompanied in their loneliness.*

Borderlines

Munawwar Abdulla

The desert here refers to the Teklimakan Desert, a shifting sand desert in the southwest of East Turkistan. Folk stories say there are ancient buried cities under it, or that the name means "once you go in, you'll never get out". Some of the oasis cities surrounding the desert comprises the term Altishahr, or "Six Cities", which is another name that refers to our homeland, particularly the Tarim Basin region in the south.

I live on borderlines and subliminal spaces,
a scion of life on the edges,
or perhaps a central intersection
jealously defined as peripheral

My home is where my heart is,
scattered through the sands
of a desert I have never seen,
the algorithms where I can never be.
My heart is a light fractured
into the colours of a rainbow,
split across the edges of the world where
the blood of my ancestors coursed with power,
familiar.

Home is a travelling being;
where I am light, she is music.
Where I am colour, she is the cry of happiness,
that shades my hues into tides,
sometimes peaceful, other times frightful,
always magnificent.

Yet, all the while,
I walk the lines between
societies, between tongues,
and bridge those countless hyphens
and wonder why
the turmoil of self-identity has been thrust into a spotlight.
Could we just be, without identifying?
How many schemas must I fill before
I become my own?

I live on borderlines and peripheries
A descendent of transference
and the welcoming of difference
An omnidirectional white light
Where home calls
in the form of
every stretched horizon
and every playful whirl of the wind
I breathe in

Homecoming

Sonya Imin

Homecoming is an intimate reflection on displacement, belonging, and the collective human search for home, influenced by my own identity negotiations as an Uyghur American person. This multi-media video and sculpture installation journeys through disjointed imagery of domestic spaces projected upon a burnt faceless bust, following a lullaby that my own mother once sang.

Uyghur Eagle Hunter

Malik Orda Turdush

Conversation
with Contributor

This work was inspired by Uyghur culture, history, and my grandfather who used to hunt with an eagle. My mother used to tell me about the eagle her father had when she was little, for hunting. He would ride off on his horse with the eagle on his arm and return with rabbits and other small game. Stories like this affected me from a young age, and bringing them to life is an amazing feeling.

ئۈمىد خەتتى

سەھەسەتووا زۇلمسرا
بەختىيار قىزى

ئۈمىد خەتتى ئۇيغۇرنىڭ ھۆنەر - ئىلىم چىرىغى بار،
ئانا يۇرتتا ئىمىز قالدۇرغان سىزىقى بار.
خەلقنىڭ مۆڭى ئىچرە ئايدىڭ تۇرغان،
ھىلال ئاي ۋە مەڭگۈ يانغان يۇلتۇزى بار.

قۇدرەتلىك ئوغۇزخان نەسلىدۇر ئۇيغۇر،
ساز ۋە مۇقام قەلبىنىڭ ۋەسلىدۇر ئۇنىڭ.
تا ئەبەد ۋەتەننىڭ ئىشقىدا يانغان،
ئۈمىد ئوتى كۆيدۇرمەس پەرۋانە ئۇيغۇر.

بەرداشلىق ئەۋلادنىڭ دۇئاسى چەكسىز،
قەلغاچقا ئۆتكۈر، لۆتپۈل روھلىرى دەۋەت.
ياڭرىغان مۆڭلۈق كۈيلەر تارمىنى بويلاپ،
جەڭگىۋار ياشقا بەرەر ئىرادە، مەدەت.

بىزنىمۇ كەزدۈرەر ھىجران خىياللار
قەشقەر، غۇلجا، ئاتۇش، تۇرپان، يورۇڭقاشقا.
ئانا تۇپراق ھەمدى قىلار نىبردىن مەھلىيا،
مەھمۇت، يۇسۇپ، ساتۇق بۆغرا ياتقان جايلارغا.

ئەجرىڭگە قاندۇرغان چاڭقاق دىللارنى،
مىننەتدار ۋارىسلار ياد ئىتەر ھامان.
ۋاز كەچمەس بولسىمۇ بۇ ۋەھشى ئازاپ،
ئابدۇخالىق ئۇيغاتقان روھى بار ئەۋلاد.

زوردۇن سابىر

مەرھۇم ئاتاقلىق يازغۇچى زوردۇن سابىرنىڭ «ئانا يۇرت» رومانىدىن پارچە.

مەكتەپنىڭ بېغى ئەجەبمۇ كۆڭۈللۈك، قېلىن قارىباغاچلىقلار، قوچاق يەتكۈسىز تەرەكلەر شاخلىرىدىكى قاغىلارنىڭ توللىشقى، خۇددى دۇنيادىكى ھەممە قاغىلار شۇ يەرگە توپلانغاندەك. سۈپسۈپياڭلارنىڭ، گۆگۆكلارنىڭ يېقىملىق ئاۋازلىرى، يۇگۇرۇشۇپ يۈرگەن ياۋا تۇشقانلارچۇ تېخى؟ بۇ باغ رەۋايەتلەردىكى سىرلىق ئورمانلىققا ئوخشايدۇ. باغنىڭ ئۇتتۇرىسىدىكى ئۆستەڭچۇ تېخى. ئۆننىڭ بويلىرىدىكى قاپاق تەرەكلەر بۇ قاشادىن – ئۇ قاشاغا يېتەلۆالغان، ئۇ ھەم كۆۋرۈك، ھەم ئىلەڭگۈچ. غولى كاۋاكشغان تەرەكلەر ئارىسىدىكى ئاق ئۇجمىچۇ؟ ئۇ بەلكى نەچچە يۈز يىلدىن بېرى مېۋە بېرىپ كېپلەۋاتقاندۇر. قويۇق ئالمىلىقلار ئارىسىدىكى چىمەنلىك تېخىمۇ كۆڭۈللۈك، ياتساڭ كۆرپە، مۇللاق ئاتساڭ مامۇق، ئۈگدا يېتىپ ئاسمانغا قارىساڭ بىر سىرلىق دۇنيا...

– بۇنداق باغ شەھەردىمۇ يوق، – دېدى سەبخە. ئۇ ئەمدىلا ئون بەش ياشقا كىرگەن، تولىمۇ چىرايلىق، ئۈزۈن يەڭلىك ئاق كۆپتىسىدىن كۆكرەكلىرى ئەمدىلا بىلىنىشكە باشلىغان، ئۈزۈن ئىككى ئۆرۈمە چېچى ھەم توم، ھەم يالتىراپ تۇرىدىغان زىلۆا قىز ئىدى، – مەن بۇ باغنى ياخشى كۆرىمەن. بۇ باغ چاربباغقا ئوخشايدۇ.

– راست، – دېدى نۇرى قىزنىڭ ئۇماق، قىپقىزىل لەۋلىرىگە تەلمۈرۈپ قاراپ چاقچاق ئارىلاش، – بۇ باغ چاربباغنىڭ ئۆزى، سەنەم جانىم چاربباغلار خاس ئىككەنىن بىلمەدىم!... دېگەن مۆشۈ بولسا كېرەك.

– ۋېيىيەي! – قىز ئانار دانىسىدەك قىزىرىپ يەرگە قارىدى، – ئۈنداق دېسەڭىز قېچىپ كېتىمەن بىكار!

نۇرى خىجىل بولۇپ يېنىدا ئېقىۋاتقان ئۆستەڭگە قارىۋالدى. ئېگىلگەن سۆگەت شاخلىرى چېچەك سۈيى بىلەن تولۇپ، شوخلىنىپ ئېقىۋاتقان سارغۇچ سۈنى تويماي سۆيىمەكتە، بۇك دەرەخلەر ئارىسىدىن گۆرردە كۆتۈرۈلگەن قۇشقاچلار ئۈلارنىڭ بېشىدىكى قېرى قارىباغاچ شېخىدا بەس – بەستە ۋىچىرلاشماقتا، ئاشقىنى تولا چىللاپ چارچىغان زەينەپ «كاككۈك كا... كا... كاككۈك كا» دەپ ھارغىن ئاۋازدا نالە قىلماقتا. مانا نەدىدۇر ئايغىر ئەسەبىلىك بىلەن كىشنىدى، تەرەكلەرنىڭ تۆپە شاخلىرىدىكى غورالداي، قۇرغۇي، كۆكنەكلەر چۇرقۇراشتى،

كەپتەرلەر كۆپكۆك ئاسمان قەرىدە گۇل چىقىرىپ پەرۋاز قىلىشتى. ئىيۇل ئېيىننىڭ ھەممە گۈزەللىكى گويا شۇ دەقىقىدىلا ئۆزىنى كۆرسەتتى، ئىنسانغا راھەت – پاراغەت بەرشىكىلا ئۆزىنى بېغىشلىغان ئۆلۈغ تەبىئەت ئۆز پەرزەنتلىرىنى نىمىشقىدۇر پۈتۈن مۆھەببىتى بىلەن ئالقىشلىدى. نۇرىننىڭ تومۇرلىرىدا گويا قان ئەمەس، ئوت ئاقتى، ئۇنىڭ يۈرىكى شۇ دەقىقىدە بىر پارچە چوغقا ئايلاندى، ۋۇجۇدى گويا بىر كۆچۈلۈك چاقماق ئۇرۇلغاندەك سىلكىندى. ئۇ ھاياتتا مىسلى كۆرۈلمىگەن ھاياجانلىق ھىسسىيات قاينىمىدا ھوشسىزلاندى، ئۇنىڭ تىلى ئۇرىنىڭ ئەسەس، ئۆزىنىڭ سۆزىمەنلىكى، باتۇرلۇقى، جاسارىتى كۆلگە ئايلاندى. ئۇ يەرگە قاراپ تۇرۇپ يىڭى تىلى چىققان بالىدەك دۇدۇقلىدى:

– ... ياق ... سىز سەبخە...

ئۇنىڭ بۇ گېپىگە بالىنىڭ ئۇمىدسىزلىكى نامرات ئارزۇلىرىنىڭ نابۇت بولۇۋاتقانلىقى، ئۇنسىز نالە – پەريادى سىڭگەنىدى. ئۇ باي قىز بىلەن نامرات ئوغۇلنىڭ ئارىسىدا ئورتاق خۇشاللىق بولمايدۇ، پەقەت پاجىئەلا بولىدۇ، نامراتلار ئارزۇسى بايلارنىڭ ۋۇجۇدىغا يات، شىبرىن خىيال بىلەن خۇشال بولۇشقا ئادەتلەنگەن، سەبخە بىلەن ئابدۇمەر مەڭبىگىنىڭ بىغىدا ئەمەس، بەلكى بىر ئۆمۈر خىيال بىغىدىلا بىللە بولاي، دىگەنلەرنى ئويلىدى – دە، ۋاقىتسىز سۆنگەن گۈل بەرگىدەك سۆلشىپ:

– مەن كېتەي، – دېدى.

– تېخى ئەتتىگەن، – دېدى قىز چىچىنىڭ ئۇچىنى چوۋۇپ تۇرۇپ، – يۇرۇڭ، ئۈچمە يەيلى، ئاندىن كېيىن سورايدىغانلىرىم بار تېخى.

ئۇ قىزغا ئەگىشىپ ئەيمىنىپ مېڭىپ قېرى ئۇجمىنىڭ تۆۋۆگە كەلدى. شاخلار شىبرىن ئۇجمە بىلەن تولغان، يەرمۇ دەسسەگۈسىز ئۇجمە. ئۇلار يەردىن ئەڭ پاكىز، شىرىنلىكلىرىنى تېرىپ يېدى.

– ئۇچىغا چىقىپ ئۇزۇپ يەيلىلا، قاراڭا، قارغۇجلار جىبىدا شىبخىدىكىنى يەۋۇاتىدۇ. ھا – ھا – ھا... – دەپ كۈلدى.

ئۇنىڭ كۆلكىسى شۇنچىلىك يىقىملىق – گويا تەمبۇرنىڭ ئاۋازى، شۇنچىلىك زىل – جانان چىننىڭ ئاۋازى، شۇنداق سىرلىق – گويا تېپىشماق ئىدى.

نۇرى قىزنىڭ بىر يەرىگە بەدىنى تېگىپ كەتسە خۇددى چوغ تېگىپ كۆيۈپ كېتىدىغاندەك ئۆزىنى قاچۇرۇپ، دەرەخ غولىغا يامىشىپ يۈقىرىغا ئۆرلىدى. قىزمۇ

يالاڭ ئاياغ بولسۇبلمپ شاخلارغا يامىشمپ ئۇنىڭ يىنىدىلا ئۆرلىمەكتە. نۇرى ئۇچ ئاچىماق شاخقا ئولتۇرۇۋېلىپ شىرنىسى ئۇرغۇپ تۇرىدىغان ئۈجمە دانىلىرىنى تېرىپ ئالمىشىغا تولدۇردى. بۇنداق شىرنىلىك، مەرۋايىتتەك يالتىراپ تۇرىدىغان مېۋىنى قانداقمۇ ئاغزىغا سالسۇن؟ ئۇ كىچىكىدىنلا ياخشى مېۋە كۆرسە ئاپىسىغا ياكى ئۇكىسىغا بېرىشكە ئادەتلەنگەن، ئۇ ئىختىيارسىز ھالدا تۆۋەنگە قاريدى. ئۇنىڭ تۆۋەنگە قارىشى بىلەن قىزنىڭ يۈقىرىغا قارىشى بىرلا ۋاقىتتا توغرا كەلدى. ئۇ قىزنىڭ ئۆزىگە تىكىلگەن يالقۇنلۇق كۆزلىرى، كۆلۈمسىرەپ تۇرغان لەۋلىرىگە چەكسىز لەززەت، ۋەھىمە ۋە تەشنالىق بىلەن قاريدى – دە، قىزىرىپ – ھودۇقۇپ قولىدىكى ئۈجمىنى قىزغا سۇندى. قىزنىڭ قوللىرى شاختا ئىدى، قىز ئاغزىنى ئاشتى. نۇرى ئۈجمىنى ئۇنىڭ ئۇماق ئاغزىغا ساناپ تۇرۇپ بىر تالدىن سىلمۆندى، ۋۇجۇدى بەختتىن گويا شامالدا نازغمغان تال چىۋقىدەك تىترىدى...

"Ana Yurt" is a trilogy of historical fiction novels by Zordun Sabir set in East Turkistan. The novels follow the life of an ensemble cast of characters, including a teenage boy, Nuri, navigating his way through a country steeped in political turmoil. It is set in the 1930s and 1940s during and after the establishment of the second East Turkistan Republic. The trilogy was one of the most popular works of Uyghur literature before being banned. This excerpt finds Nuri in Chapter 2 of the first book with the daughter of a government official. Earlier, the government official had summoned Nuri to explain a letter of complaint his small village had asked Nuri to write...

     UNDER THE MULBERRY TREE

Ana Yurt

Zordun Sabir

Translation | Munawwar Abdulla

The mingbeg's orchard was emphatically blissful. It was thick with elm trees, and it seemed like all the crows in the world had gathered on the large poplars that scattered throughout. The beautiful songs of orioles and cuckoos hung in the air, and wild rabbits hopped about in delight. Being in this orchard felt like stepping into the magical forests of fairy tales. A stream ran through its centre. The calabashes growing on its banks extended from one side to the other, creating both a bridge and a natural swing. White mulberries grew from under the hollowed trunks of poplar trees; they had probably been fruiting there for hundreds of years. The meadows amongst the thick brushes of apple trees were even more heavenly; to sleep there was to be blanketed, to roll on the ground was to roll on down feathers, to lay there and look at the sky was to be in an enchanted world…

"Even the city does not have this sort of orchard," said Sebihe. She was a beautiful, slender girl who had recently turned fifteen, only just showing signs of womanhood through her white blouse, with two long, thick braids glittering down her back. "I love this orchard. It looks like a Charbagh."

"True," said Nuri, looking longingly at the girl's cute, red lips. He half jokingly went on, "this orchard is a Charbagh. So that's what they must have meant when they said, *Senem my dear, I had not been aware, you are of the gardens of Eden!*"

"Oh my!" Sebihe looked down, turning red as a pomegranate seed, "I will leave if you talk like that!"

Embarrassed, Nuri looked away to the nearby stream. The bending willow tree branches, filled with blossom dew, were forever kissing the frolicking, pale gold water. The flurry of birds fluttering up from dense thickets competed in song in front of the branches of an old elm tree. The zeynep bird, tired from calling out to her lover, sighed an exhausted "cuckkook ka… ka… cuckkook". A stallion whinnied with nervousness from a location unknown. The ghoralday, sparrowhawks, and falcons began to clamour from the highest branches of the poplar trees, and pigeons soared into the depths of the blue heavens in formations of flowers. It was as if all the splendours of July had made themselves apparent in that second. Venerable Nature, who had devoted itself to giving peace and comfort to humanity, for reasons unknown, applauded its children with an all-encompassing love. The blood in Nuri's veins was no longer blood, but fire. His heart in that moment had turned to ember and his spirit shook as if struck by a powerful bolt of lightning. He faltered in the unprecedented whirlpool of excited emotions; his tongue was no longer his own, his eloquence, his courage, his bravery turned to ash. He looked at the ground and stuttered like a child who had just begun to speak.

"No… Sebihe…"

His voice had become effused with the hopelessness of youth, the slow destruction of his destitute desires, a silent lament. Rich girls and poor boys could not share happiness, only tragedy. The hopes of the destitute were foreign to the spirits of the rich, and sweet fantasies were a fruitless tree. "I am used to being content with my imagination. Sebihe and Abdumar can be together not in the mingbeg's orchard, but perhaps just in my mind forever," Nuri thought. He wetted and extended a prematurely fallen flower.

"I should leave," he said at last.

"It's still early," said the girl, twirling the ends of her braids, "Come, let's eat some mulberries, and I still want to ask you some questions."

He timidly followed the girl to the foot of the ancient mulberries. The branches were thick with the sweet fruit, and the surrounding floor was covered with it. They picked the cleanest, juiciest ones from the ground and ate.

"Why don't we climb up to the top and pick them from the tree. Look, the starlings are eating them straight from the branches for all they're worth!" the girl laughed.

Her laugh was as lovely as a tambur, beautiful and melodious, like the ring of fine porcelain, yet mysterious, like a riddle.

Nuri distanced himself from her, as if accidentally touching her would burn him, and climbed atop the tree. The girl followed suit, going barefoot to climb up next to him. Nuri sat himself between three branches and gathered the juiciest looking mulberries. But he couldn't simply eat such titillating, pearl-like mulberries. Ever since he was little, he would give the best fruit to his mother or younger brother. Out of habit, he glanced below and caught her eyes. He looked at those blazing eyes and smiling lips with infinite pleasure, fear, and yearning, and, blushing, extended the mulberries to her. She opened her mouth, her hands fixed to the branches of the tree. Nuri carefully placed the mulberries, one by one, in her mouth, and his entire being shook from happiness like a single twig being tossed by the wind…

Credits

POETRY

Muyesser Abdul'ehed (Hendan)

Munawwar Abdulla

Aykezar Adil

Jangul Baurjan

Mirshad Ghalip

Mutellip Iqbal

Aynur Korla

Zulmira Magametova

Abdushukur Muhammet

Zohre Uyghur

PROSE

Merdan Eheteli

Yadykar Ibraimov

Maidina Kadeer

Elminur Mahpirof

Kabir Qurban

Ali Sibir

Manzire

VISUAL ART

Dilshat Aripov

Ablikim Bughra

Camilla Dilshat

İlminur Efvan

Ayesha Erkin

Sonya Imin

Subi Imam

Aynur Korla

Leena Kuerban

Sarvenaz Nurali

Sarah Suzuk

Malik Orda Turdush

TRANSLATORS

Munawwar Abdulla

Joshua L. Freeman

Mirshad Ghalip

Heyrinsa Memetsidiq Izchi

Tumaris Yalqun

EDITORIAL TEAM

Munawwar Abdulla

Sonya Imin

Maidina Kadeer

Emily Zinkin

DESIGN & SUPPORT TEAM

Arfat Erkin

Jodie Manning

Shiffa Samad

Eleanor Wilson

THE TARIM NETWORK

The Tarim Network is a charity based in London, United Kingdom. We are a family of passionate individuals creating a platform to unite, inspire, and advance the Uyghur youth in diaspora. Our mission is to create a global Uyghur youth community that inspires and cultivates excellence while providing cultural and social enrichment for its members.
www.thetarimnetwork.com

RENÉ CASSIN

René Cassin is a charity working to promote and protect universal human rights, drawing on Jewish experience and values. We achieve this by campaigning for change and building the capacity of activists to promote and protect human rights. We are named after Monsieur René Cassin, the French-Jewish Nobel Peace Laureate and co-author of the Universal Declaration of Human Rights.
www.renecassin.org

MOISHE HOUSE

Moishe House is what being Jewish in your 20s is all about. We provide a space for over 70,000 young adults around the world to create meaningful, welcoming Jewish communities for themselves and their peers.
www.moishehouse.org

The lands we dream from